Thriving Beyond the Tears

Bruised and Never Broken

Dr. Stem Mahlatini

ISBN-13: 978-1-7328275-6-1

ISBN-10: 1-7328275-6-7

Written by: Dr.Stem Sithembile Mahlatini Drstem14@gmail.com | www.drstemspeaks.com www.globalcounselingcoaching.com

Facebook: DrStem Mahlatini
Twitter: DrStemahlatini
LinkedIn: Drstem Mahlatini
Skype: Dr. Mahlatini

Foreword by: Dr.Stem Sithembile Mahlatini
Cover Design by: Phillip Mudavanhu
Book Formatting & Layout by: Masimba Mukundinashe
Photography by: Ed Pedi Photography Studio & Gardens
    North Andover, Massachusetts 01845
    978-686-6535
    www.edpediphoto.com
    email: linda@edpediphoto.com

Category: BISAC: Self-Help / Motivational & Inspirational

Library of Congress Cataloging-in-Publication Data
Printed in the USA

DrStem
Teen Parent Empowerment Seminars - TPES

About the book

"How Can We Succeed Against The Odds?"

In her powerful new book, Dr. Sithembile "Stem" Mahlatini discusses how several key traits – among them determination, goal-setting, faith, and forgiveness – can allow even the least of us to succeed beyond our wildest dreams. Part memoir, part inspirational column,

THRIVING BEYOND THE TEARS is Dr. Stem's way of opening dialogue among victims of domestic violence, women and children of polygamy, those with a traumatic upbringing that has held them back and those who find themselves stuck and unable to move beyond their tears. After all when we hang in there, there is Joy and Peace Beyond The Tears, because no matter what hand you are dealt in life, there will be a way to live a fulfilling life.

Thriving Beyond the Tears
Dedication to My Dad

"How true Daddy's words were when he said: 'All children must look after their own upbringing.' Parents can only give good advice or put them on the right paths, but the final forming of a person's character lies in their own

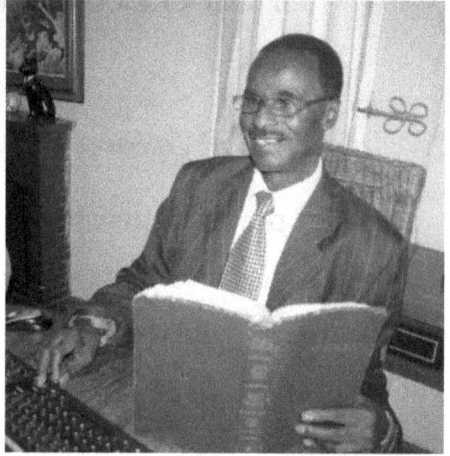

hands." -- Anne Frank, German Jew and Holocaust Victim.

Dad you did the best that you could and I choose to remember and acknowledge those moments where you loved us unconditionally, provided for us unconditionally and guided us with greatness and essence. I will forever be grateful for all your sacrifices and belief in your children's strengths, you always wanted the best for us. I thank you for paving the path and believing in me to lead the family to even greater heights. - I love you daddy.

Love Always Stem

Thriving Beyond the Tears
Dedication to My Mum

Abraham Lincoln said, "All that I am and all that I ever hope to be, I owe to my mother." I am proud to dedicate this Book to my Mother, Idah Sanganza-Mahlatini, who has been my strength, my motivator and my number one supporter.

It is your tears I hope to honor, Mother. Thank you for continuing to pray for me. God is Able. I am honored to be in your presence because I learn more and more of your strength every day. May hope, joy and happiness be yours, beyond your tears. May all those whom you minister also find their true selves and happiness through your testimonies.

I love you, Mommy.

Thriving Beyond the Tears
CONTENTS:

Thriving Beyond the Tears - *Bruised and Never Broken* | Dr. Stem Mahlatini

Acknowledgements

I would like to thank my parents, Benjamin and Idah Mahlatini. I also wish to thank my siblings and their spouses: Sithabile & Peter Kahari; Sidumile & Fungai Marange; Sibusisiwe & Philip Ruffen; Stanley and his wife Brenda Mahlatini, Simon and his wife Svetlana and son Jayden (our legacy), Sinikiwe (Nikkie) and her soon-to-be-husband Teddy "Q" Valcourt, Simon and his family.

To my nieces, my nephews, my Mahlatini siblings, my Nyagura and Sanganza relatives, and the current and former students and staff of Salem High School in Massachusetts, this book is both an acknowledgment and proof that you are bigger than your circumstances, bigger than what people say about you.

To my Coach and Mentor, Linda Eastman, I will forever be grateful for the opportunity to be a part of Professional Woman Network, prowoman.net. I am also indebted to my trusted friends, advisors and editors, Dr. John Loblack, Susan Shepherd, and my good friend Frank

Kashner. I thank my good friend Saru Furusa Walsh for the wonderful memories and unconditional friendship, and I would also like to thank Ruru Mkonto, Eliza McCall Horne, Elisabeth Avila, Evelyn Lauture, Carol McFarlane, Melanie Favors, Paulette Randolph, Rhonda Scott, Lee Furusa, Rose Shenje, Mai Mabara, Sharon Kanyangarara and Salvador Lainez.

A special, heartfelt thank you to My Beloved Ernst "Ernie" Louis. Thank you for teaching and showing me the true meaning of unconditional love, what to expect from a true, kind, loving, gentle, dedicated, trustworthy husband and best friend.

To all of you unyielding readers and supporters, I will forever be grateful. Thank you for your continued support, good thoughts and prayers.
To Steve Muzite and the staff at Visions FM, thank you for the opportunity to be a presenter at Visions FM Radio. I never knew I would love radio this way; I love music and talking so I guess it was meant to be. Thank you.

THE VOICE OF HOPE
-Stem

Foreword

As of this publication, I do not have to walk on eggshells anymore. I can be myself. I can make my own decisions and my own choices. I do not need to make anyone's opinion of me or of my choices determine who I become. I am free.

There are no limits; the sky is not even a limit, and I can be who I want to be and do anything I want to do in divine order. There are no limitations to my happiness, my joy, my blessings, my possibilities, or my life. Zero limits. This is my hope and prayer for you, the reader.

I am delivered from the power of fear, lack, or anxiety. No weapon formed against me shall prosper. Doors of abundance, prosperity, eternal happiness, business, family, and success are now open to me.

The Lord has not given me a spirit of fear, but of power and of love and of a sound mind. I now love myself unconditionally. I give myself love. I open myself to the

11

possibilities of life. It is so sweet to trust in Jesus, just to take him at his word.

Abraham Lincoln said, "All that I am and all I ever hope to be, I owe to my mother." I say, "All that I am and all I ever hope to be, I owe to my father and mother, Benjamin and Idah Mahlatini, whom I dedicate this book to. Their love and guidance have made me all that I am and enable all that I ever hope to be. Because of them, I learned to lead, to dream, to live big, and to believe that all dreams come true.

I would also like to dedicate this book to all children of polygamy, and to the wives of polygamy, those strong women who have struggled as single parents. I dedicate this book to those women and youth who are struggling to get back up and be someone, to those who dare to dream big and believe in miracles despite their circumstances.

I now know what Les Brown was talking about when he said, "Someone's opinion of you does not have to become your reality. ... Regardless of your circumstances you can succeed. Regardless of where you were born, who your parents are, your demographic area or your economical background you can succeed."My hope is to instill this same message to you, the reader, and to all people that I will encounter in this lifetime.

Introduction

Imagine that you wake up to discover that your husband has brought another woman to live with your family in your own home. She sleeps in the next room. From where you are, you can see them going into the bedroom, hear them make love, laugh, and carry on, while you cry yourself to sleep every night.

Imagine the sleepless nights, the heavy heart, the pain, the heart-to-heart talks and prayers with God that begin to seem meaningless as you live out this unending nightmare ... for years. Worse, the woman gets pregnant several times in your home, and you are forced to care for her and her children. Your once-beautiful marriage crumbles under your feet.... It's over; he doesn't love you anymore.

He doesn't respect you anymore, so he brings another woman into your home. You have seven children to raise; you contemplate leaving, but what about the children?

How would they feel; how would they live? Would they be taken care of? Would they understand why you had to leave? These were questions my mother had to ask herself when she found herself faced with my father's decision to become a polygamist.

This is what my mother, a woman of God, a beloved daughter, endured when my father, decided to marry a second wife and bring the woman into my mother's home to stay. Polygamy is an acceptable practice in Zimbabwe, Africa, where I am from. The focus of my memoir is not on polygamy or whether it is an acceptable or unacceptable practice.

My focus is on the effects that it has on the human emotion, on the wives, on the children who are born or raised in a polygamist family, and the long-term effects it has on all parties. The pain is unbearable, and many have not had the opportunity to openly talk about the pain or about the long-term effects they have suffered as a result.

It's time the pain is voiced. It's time my mother speaks from her heart and frees herself from the emotional turmoil she has unnecessarily endured for many years. It's time we, the children, speak out about our own lives' complexities and the pains we have suffered as well.

At long last, it's time to explore what lies Thriving Beyond the tears. The pains and struggles I write of here are similar to many of the struggles that others have faced in their own lives, particularly the hidden inner pain of childhood traumas that shape who we become as we grow into adults.

These are unspoken, deeper pains that we all face as children. When we become adults, nobody else knows about what we endured ... until something tragic happens. Then everyone wonders what happened.

It took me months and months of prayer for the courage to start this book. I feared what the world would say, and most importantly, how my father would react to this book. I feared his retaliation, and feared he would not see the love and respect that we, his children, and our mother feel for him.

Our wish is to heal so that we can then let it be. Recently, I learned that my mother was ready to openly talk about her pains, her experiences, for the first time, without fear of being ridiculed or rejected. Many tears were shed over the years, many hearts were broken, and many spirits were dampened and disheartened.

The challenge is that my father is totally closed and unwilling to talk to his wife, my mother, let alone to his family, about the challenges and pains caused by his choice to live a polygamist lifestyle.

My mother is also unwilling to speak to my father about her pains because she fears retaliation. On the other hand, being a psychotherapist, I have many times wanted to sit down with both my parents and talk. But requesting that we sit down and discuss anything to do with a parent's choice is seen as disrespectful in my culture.

The man is a domineering figure in the family, so for most women and children, the pain caused by polygamist relationships has gone unnoticed and unspoken. Even though the man is the one who is the root cause of the emotional pains of polygamy, he is also the one who has had the choice of whether or not to allow the conversation to happen.

Will he make room for a heart-to-heart talk that will allow healing and clear the air? It is also time for the man involved to speak about their struggles (I believe there are) of being in this position of being a husband and father to many. My father at first when I first wrote the first version of this book was no different; when asked, he was visibly and verbally very angry and defensive, causing more pain than there was before.

I found that during the many times I had tried to talk to my father, he stated that he felt like I was confronting him, questioning him about his actions, and yet mine was an attempt for me to understand and express my pains and the struggle I had endured because of his polygamy and what I saw as betrayal of our family.

Looking back yes I see why it was confrontational because in my tradition, as a daughter I am not allowed to ask or discuss my parents' marital issues o status. "ndezvevakuru" is what I grew up hearing, meaning this was not for the children. During these attempted moments of discussion, words were exchanged, and consequently, much was said that inflicted more pain, anger and resentment upon all parties.

I have since left it alone, and choose to love my parents, yes both equally as you will read in this memoir. I now understand at 50, that there is way much more that goes on between two people that the world, even us children will never understand. Thriving beyond the tears, the choice is all ours, we get to choose how we live thriving beyond the tears.

I am so excited I get to map out and choose how I will live my life: encouraging and empowering others to take a really good at what's limiting them, what's getting in the way of achieving a joy filled successful life. My healing and this book means I am Free to help others including yourself to choose forgiveness, joy, peace and love, through my coaching, counselling, seminars, television/radio shows and books.

This book is my way of opening a dialogue among the many children of polygamy and wives of polygamy; children, men, and women with a painful past. I would like to help us all to bring closure to the pain we have suffered. I hope that this book will inspire and empower all who read it to believe in themselves, to declare that although their past may have bruised them, still they are not broken.

This book can be one way to finally allow us to open ourselves up to new life ventures, to take back the power and faith we need to rebuild and create a great life for ourselves now and in the future.

All of the chapters are written with helpful tools that will be a guide to help you move from pain to healing, from anger, resentment, and hatred, to forgiveness.

During more than twenty years as a licensed psychotherapist, I have worked with many individuals, families and groups who have endured childhood and marital traumas, among other possible ailments.

Somehow, I always managed to suppress my own inner struggles, even though they have stood in the way of me living my own best life. I hope that this will be a way for all those loving wives, husbands, mothers and children to begin healing, because healing is necessary for us to be able to move on and to pursue the lives we were meant to live.

1

The Early Years
- Born to Lead

Train up a child in the way he should go; even

when he is old he will not depart from it.

(Proverbs 22:6 ESV)

Thriving Beyond the Tears - *Bruised and Never Broken* | Dr. Stem Mahlatini

Chapter 1
The Early Years
- Born To Lead

Y ou are a leader; when you do well, everyone will do well. Your brothers and sisters look up to you and your family is depending on you to carry the family's name." These were the words my parents bombarded me with during my early childhood growing up in the Kambuzuma Township of Zimbabwe. I am the first of seven children, five girls and two boys; the firstborn of proud parents Idah Sanganza Mahlatini and Benjamin Mahlatini. My parents were married in 1965.

At that time, we lived in a one-room house in Mbare, and then moved to a two-room home in Kambuzuma Township. As I reflect back on those early days, I can still see the house; it holds many special memories of my formative years.

Those were often difficult days, but my mother was determined to groom her children for the challenges of tomorrow. Although we did not have much, we never went hungry.

As a young child, I did not understand the gravity of our circumstances enough to appreciate my mother's handling of the situation. Looking back, I now sympathize with my mother, but boy, to me she seemed like a mean old lady.

As children, we suffered the wrath of my mother for even the slightest infraction. My mother did not spare the rod; she believed that to save the child and raise fine, upstanding people, she needed to use the rod to correct us. For example, I remember being whipped on one occasion for refusing to take off my Physical Education Uniform.

In spite of the soundness of my reason, my mother was adamant about rules and regulations. We were supposed to remove our school uniforms immediately after school. That day, however, I was celebrating my school's victory in an athletic competition, and had worn my school uniform after school as a gesture of support. Yet my mother would not have any of that. She was afraid that I would destroy the one uniform that I had.

After all, there was no money to buy a replacement uniform if the one I was wearing was destroyed. Today, however, I understand my mother's frustrations. I understand her anger; she was prepared to do everything possible to protect the little that we had.

She did not want to have to spend the few dimes she had to her name to replace a uniform that was damaged because of my juvenile indiscretions. Her reaction to my behavior could also be chalked up to her pride. She did not want her neighbors to know that we were poor.

Our plight kept my mother crying day in and day out as she struggled to raise her children. As we grew older, my siblings and I would walk through the neighborhood selling mangoes, bananas and oranges. Although my mother tells me how quiet I was as a child, I remember making my contribution to the upkeep of the family.

Throughout our struggles, my mother constantly reminded me about the importance of education. She used to say, "If you do not do well in school, you will become a nobody."

She made me feel that I had no choice but to do well academically because I wanted to be somebody. It wasn't easy, but I worked as hard as I possibly could to make it.

As I write these words, an incident jumps out at me. It was a rainy day, and because we had no transportation at our disposal we had to walk to school. In our household, as I've mentioned, education was seen as our ticket to a better life. Unfortunately, by the time we got to school, we were drenched and our teachers denied us entry into the classroom.

As wet as we were, we felt like we were involuntarily imprisoned in the bathroom where we were told to stay until we dried up before we could go back in class. We attempted wringing our uniforms dry, the only way we knew how, but it did not work. I asked my sister Star about this incident and she remembered it like yesterday.

We haven't talked about it in a long time, but sure enough we both cried as we recalled the incident. We were sad and embarrassed because we were the only ones who were sitting in the bathroom trying to dry ourselves. When we shared our experience with our mother, she was devastated. At the time, she was—and still is—a praying woman; a woman who believes that God will have mercy on her family.

Her faith, I believe, enabled her to give us a solid, principled foundation on which to grow. We were and still are a praying family; a family that benefited from my mother's strong and unwavering faith. One of my mother's favorite prayers was, "Lord, let my tears be a blessing to my children," hence the Book Title: Thriving Beyond the Tears—Bruised and Never Broken.

In Shona it is pronounced, *"Misodzi yangu ngaive chipo kuvana vangu."*

I took those words literally and have always believed that there is nothing I cannot do because my path was prayed for and anointed by my mother's words. My involvement in church and community activities kept me focused on the positive things that life had to offer.

I was an altar girl, I participated in Sunday school, I served as a youth leader and I became a member of the Girls' Brigade. My involvement in these activities helped me tremendously. They opened my eyes to what might one day be, instead of the harsh reality of my family's poverty. While we were in Kambuzuma, we went to bed most evenings after consuming porridge and chicken feet when my father was not home.

I remember those days you could get a big slice of meat for 20 cents and we would cut that one piece into many pieces to make stew. I remember Mother loved sending me to the butcher because I was so friendly that whenever I went, I brought back a larger piece than my siblings.

To expand our menu and improve upon our plight, Mother started growing corn and sweet potatoes and offering them for sale. My sisters would think I have selective memory if I do not mention that our first attempt at entrepreneurship as children started with us selling mangoes on the streets in Kambuzuma. I remember us yelling "Mangoes!" together and feeling very sad, embarrassed and defeated when we didn't sell much.

My sister Star was very persistent, but I was shy and easily embarrassed and did not want anything to do with selling mangoes on the street. I did not want anything to do with being in the fields, either. So my mother always used to tell me that I had better get educated, as I would amount to nothing otherwise, since I did not want to sell food or be a worker in the corn fields.

I laugh today because it's true today I don't enjoy being in the corn fields, I however love selling. I guess because I have worked hard to overcome my shyness, I am able to sell anything—I bet you I can sell you more mangoes than you anticipate buying if I sold you the mangoes today. Yes, my intention is to make sure I now sell at a higher scale than when I sold produce on the streets of Kambuzuma.

But I learned some of my marketing skills back then, even though my shyness might have made me appear distanced from it all. I love a plaque in my home that reads, "Everything I have learned, I learned from my mother," Author Unknown. Indeed, if Mother had not pushed us to

28

sell, we all would not have the business skills we have today; they don't teach real life experience in business school.

My sister has gone on to own her own very successful business, a Beauty Salon, Kreative Hair Design and Beauty Supply in Lynn, Massachusetts. Meanwhile, we all looked forward to the days when Dad was home. Whenever he was there, we felt we ate very well until he left home again and everything went back to not have having much.

However, it would not be much longer before things took a turn for the better. That was when Dad decided to go to a Real Estate School to become a Realtor. He was now home all the time, and it was during that time that Mother decided to learn how to knit sweaters. Although Mother came from a very prominent family, marrying my father meant that she was on her own.

In other words, she could not now seek help from her own father, Freddie Kadoko Sanganza, a former prominent businessman in the Mutare and Mbare townships. She, however, never forgot the entrepreneurial lessons she had learned from her father.

She took those lessons and opened up a sweater-knitting business of her own. Her business and Dad's real estate business did so well that we were able to change our place of residence.

We moved to a community called Waterfalls, a community in which the Mahlatini's became well known. Father for his Real Estate, Mother for knitting sweaters, and us children went on to become Top Models with Silhouettes and Zollies modeling schools before we left the country to come to the USA.

Thinking back, I believe that there is great merit in what Joyce Maynard said: "It's not only children who grow. Parents do, too. As much as we watch to see what our children do with their lives, they are watching us to see what we do with ours. I can't tell my children to reach for the sun. All I can do is reach for it."

My parents struggled, as most parents do when starting a new family. What made the difference was their belief in hard work and their faith. They believed that they could create a better life for themselves and for their family. I find myself saying, "If they could work that hard and get us out of Kambuzuma, I sure can get them to higher ground now that the tables have turned, the money is gone, and the businesses have all been closed down.

My father always said that education was power and that education opens doors. I witnessed the change in him after he became a Realtor, which was a result of education. His wish for his children was for us to go to school and wait to start a family, stating we could start a family at any time. Well, I took him seriously and being my parents' pleaser I believed family could wait or so I believed, blissfully unaware of the 'biological clock' information I learned about many years later.

My father never wanted his children to rush into marriage to escape poverty, the way so many of our friends had done. Many people will remember my sisters and me as top Zimbabwe models with Zollies and Silhouettes. Our parents enrolled us in a modeling school to keep us from going astray.

Both Mom and Dad said that being models would also help to groom us for the business world. They were right; modeling school, fashion shows, commercials, and beauty pageants all made a difference. My siblings and I all managed to divert ourselves from starting families at an early age; instead, we put our focus on pursuing education first. In Zimbabwe there is a term, "nhaka," which refers to the property or the monies that one leaves for their family when they pass on.

My parents used to constantly tell us that they had nothing to leave to us when they died. They hammered into us the importance of education, stating that it would provide the means for us to succeed. Education, they felt, was their contribution to what we would accomplish in our lives so that we could one day leave nhaka for our own children, their grandchildren.

Thriving Beyond The Tears—Bruised But Not Broken traces my humble journey. It exposes you to the road I have traveled and shows you how I have made it my mission to live a life that was fertilized by my mother's tears. It is a book that teaches you the power of prayer, resiliency, dedication, hard work, hope and faith. Let my tears be a blessing to my children was my mother's prayer, which I attribute as one of the main reasons we are all doing well today.

What follows is my story through my father's eyes, who, I have no doubt, loves all his children and probably had no indication or any clue how much pain his decisions would cause. I truly believe he had no idea that his actions would scar us, his children, for such a long time.

I grew up being Daddy's girl, but I was so hurt and

disappointed with his decision because he is the one that taught us that polygamy was a dumb idea. He said people destroy their families for nothing and yet he ended up doing the very same thing. I asked him to write me an introduction that I could include in my book, and he wrote the following heartfelt letter:

Sithembile, you were my firstborn, and from the moment you could sit down and crawl around, I knew that there was something special about you. I knew you would be a leader. At an early age, you became very responsible; you displayed leadership skills far Thriving Beyond your years.

Because of what we saw in you, your mother and I reminded you time and time again about being a leader. I was not home much to [see] how difficult it was for you and your mother, so I will tell what I remember of you from whenever I was home. I will also share with you the growth I have seen in you over the years. I am convinced, however, that others might ask, "How could an infant show leadership?"

If I were to be asked that question, I would say that leadership in children is displayed through their independence. As a child you displayed a high level of independence.

Unlike your siblings, you cried a lot, yet you would stop crying as soon as I held you in my hands. I am not sure if you did it to attract attention, my attention, but you did it as often as you could get away with it. Nonetheless, as soon as your crying episodes were over, you would immediately start arranging, destroying and rearranging the toys that were placed before you on the floor.

Other times, I would put you outside in the yard on a blanket. On the blanket, I would put some sand all around you for your comfort and protection. Then you would go round and round on the blanket playing with your toys. As poor as we were back then, we could not afford modern toys. Instead, I used sticks, tins and spoons as toys for you.

While your mother worked on her [household] chores, you would arrange, rearrange and rearrange those items. When there was no one else to play with, you were comfortable [with] playing [by] yourself. Sometimes, you would play by yourself for hours.

As I look back over the years, I remember hearing your mother yelling at the top of her voice, "Where is my daughter?" Those were the times when you went out of her sight for a brief moment. But there you were, playing quietly [by] yourself; everything would be normal again.

Away from home, you used to protect other children at school; you protected them from bullies. You were able to stop the bullies, not because of your physical power, but because of the leadership skills you possessed as a child. Those same skills are serving you well today as an adult.

I would be the first to tell you though that there was more to you than your independence; you were a prankster. You used to tease your mother and me regularly.

In addition to your aptitude for pranks, you were a very inquisitive child; you questioned everything. No matter where we were and what time of day it was, you were always awake asking question after question. You ignored the fact that everyone else was asleep.

It was then that I realized that you had a gift for speaking. You loved everyone and you were not afraid to engage anyone in conversation. You were growing into a very confident young woman.

For example, when you turned 18, I introduced you to real estate and you grasped the art of selling immediately. Because you connected easily with people, selling came easy for you.

To me, you have always been a go-getter; therefore, I wasn't surprised to learn that you were pursuing a doctoral degree. In fact, I was thrilled; I always knew you would do it.

More than that, I am so proud of who you have become and I have no doubt that you will use your background, training and experiences to educate, motivate and inspire others to live life to the fullest.

I love you. Dad."

Lessons Learned

I learned at this phase that our environment shapes who we become, but we change at any moment when our pasts no longer benefit us. Coming to America was a rude awakening because I have had to deal with a melting pot of cultures, personalities, and back grounds.

Having the flexibility to adjust, to do whatever is necessary legally to get to where you want to go is key. I know of many people that are stuck to their childhood, so they swear they will not take the necessary actions to better their lives because they do not believe in it.

I learned that parents are human too; they, too, make mistakes or rescind on their word as my father did when he married two more wives after my mother. I learned to separate my mother's jealousies and pain over this rejection so that I could move on and start my own family.

A Dose of Motivation

I want to share with you one my favourite Christian cards that I bought from a local bookstore over twenty years ago, when I came to this country. This card has gotten me through tough times, times of self-doubt and fear. I hope it will be a source of motivation to you as well.

GOD'S Promises to ...STEM

- I will never leave you nor forsake you. Joshua 1:5

- I will instruct you and teach you in the way you should go; I will counsel you and watch over you. Psalm 32:8

- I will sustain you and I rescue you. Isaiah 46:4

- I will strengthen you and help you; I will uphold you with my righteous right hand. Isaiah 41:10

- I will be with you and will watch over you wherever you go. Genesis 28:15

- I have engraved you on the palms of my hands. Isaiah 49:16

- I will walk with you and among you and be your God, and you will be my people. Leviticus 26:12

These as well as many other Bible verses strengthen me when I am weak, as I have no doubt God's handprint is all over whatever is happening to me at that moment. I am grateful for his promises, for I have learned His will and not my will be done at all times.

2

The Big Move to the USA
- Dealing with Change

"Do not follow where the path may lead. Go instead where there is no path and leave a trail." Harold R. McAlindon

Chapter 2

The Big Move to the USA
- Dealing with Change

I had heard of people leaving their homes and their countries to better their lives by seeking an education, and for the life of me, I never thought it would be possible for me. Unfortunately, when I completed my high school career with merely average grades, I was unable to get into the one local university in Zimbabwe.

I was incredibly disappointed and angry with myself for not having better grades, even though I had worked my tail off hoping to get good grades. I had to repeat my senior year in order to seek better grades, and again I failed to get accepted into the university.

In those days, most of the girls I went to school with were getting married and starting families; only a lucky few had gone on to seek a higher education. I had a boyfriend at the time who wanted very badly to get married to me, but I was not about to stop my life and become a housewife; I wanted to better my education to be a better partner to my husband, be independent and have the ability to care for myself and my family if God forbids I got divorced or my husband decided to practice polygamy. Unfortunately, I promised him I would come back and marry him after I finished school, and have stayed for over 20 years now. Yes he later married and we are best friends today he is actually my big brother as he is older than me.

I had always heard that where there is a will, there is a way. I had to seek a way to make sure I could pursue my education. My uncle who is a United Methodist Minister, Rev. Sanda Sanganza, had been in the United States a great deal while working on church missions and for education purposes.

I immediately went to him and asked for his help in applying to colleges in the United States. I wanted to come to the United States to further my education, to expand my horizons, and yes, to fulfil my inner desire of becoming more than just a mere housewife. My parents had done well and worked very hard to obtain what they had acquired by the time I left for the USA.

I wanted to be more than a young woman with average grades. I yearned to become the leader that they had deemed me from such an early age. Mother always said without fail, "what you see here is mine and my husband's hard work, this is ours. You have to work for your own", she was not kidding and we are so glad we also took her seriously.

As Confucius rightly suggests, "Wherever you go, go with all your heart." I now know, looking back, how important it is that we pursue our dreams with all our hearts. Focusing with our entire being on making the necessary changes for our own personal joy is imperative; if we are completely focused on our goal, it becomes far easier to achieve.

At some point in my life, I recognized that my life in Zimbabwe had pockets of both sad and joyful moments. My childhood was an edifying experience and offered endless challenges.

I now had to create endless opportunities for growth for myself. The power was within me, but I had to make the necessary changes and convince my parents that to have a good life I had to make it happen for myself. At one point, I believed, like most people, that my parents had to make sure I would get the best life possible.

Then, when I was rejected from the University, I thought, "Oh, well; I guess I better consider marriage and call it quits."

These were my external, immediate, reactionary thoughts, but that inner voice was so strong. I could hear it saying that I could make it, I deserved more, so I listened. Once I gave up believing that others held my joy, I breathed a sigh of relief and accepted that to better my life I had to make the right choices and act on them.

Many people I have grown to know still rely on others to make their lives better, to give them the go-ahead to make choices in their lives. I can only imagine the struggle to get free that most go through especially those who have experienced a difficult childhood and the parents are now gone. It is for this reason I write this book, to start the healing process so that you too can live your best life.

At age twenty-one, I got to choose. I chose to leave my home country of Zimbabwe and pursue an education instead of getting married and settling for being a housewife. My uncle helped me get into National College in Rapid City, South Dakota, here in the USA.

I have to say that it was so important for me to get my parents' approval and support in order to make this big change and leave home. Even though I was twenty-one, my parents decided to have my father, who had never left the country, accompany me to the USA so that he could see for himself where I was going and what life was like in a foreign place he had never seen. We arrived at National College two weeks early and were told the school was opening in two weeks, so there were only a few staff members on campus preparing for students to arrive.

My father refused to leave me if there were no other students on campus, so off we flew, back to Zimbabwe, so that I could come back with everyone else. I am also told the paperwork also needed additional information from Zimbabwe. I look at my father accompanying me not as a crazy gesture but as unconditional love from my dad, who has always been a very protective and loving father.

He probably has no idea that his and my mother's unconditional love and belief in my abilities played a big role in how I would adjust to and cope with the changes I faced when I arrived back in the USA.

One of the very first challenges I faced happened at the New York LaGuardia airport. I had come back with a whole baked chicken, rice and vegetables, because when I came with my father the local food had no taste. Because we did not have many US dollars, we survived on peanuts and ginger ale because we both love peanuts and they were cheap and tasty, so we settled for them as a meal.

So when I came back by myself and brought back my whole chicken I was not anticipating the reception I received at the airport. To my uttermost devastation, I was not allowed to come into the USA with my chicken and rice.

The immigration officers put me in a small holding room and questioned me as to why I had come into and then left the country so quickly. They also wanted to know why I was back, and why I was bringing in cooked food. This was too overwhelming and very intimidating for me; I missed my dad already.

I was given a chance to eat as much as I could in the holding room and had to trash the rest. I ate all I could and threw out the rest. This was my food for a week or two. I was devastated. Even today, I get so upset because that roasted chicken smelled and looked so good. My mother and my late aunt Dorothy Mahlatini-Chisvo had cooked it for me, and those officers made me throw it out.

Oh well such is life in these United States of America. After 911 I understand the need for such stringent rules regarding food being brought in the country.

My next immediate challenge that I won't forget was during my second week at the school, when I found a job on campus in the business office that paid $2.50 an hour. I was elated that I could work, because at this time, besides tuition, my parents had difficulty getting foreign currency.

My excitement did not last long. I was called by the business manager in her office. She told me what a good worker I was; however, people in the office were concerned about the odour I had. I smelled really bad, she said. If I were Caucasian like her I would have turned red, I was so shocked. I was hurt, too, but most of all I was embarrassed.

She asked what kind of shampoo I used and the name of the soap, and when I told her the brands I was using, which were from Zimbabwe, she quickly said I had to change and buy something from the USA because they would smell better.

The problem: I had no money. So, with tears in my eyes, I told her I had no money and would have none until I got paid. She offered to buy me the soap, perfume, and shampoo I needed. As much as I was grateful, my self-esteem was now very, very low.

Not only was I struggling to acclimate myself to this new environment now I had to worry about bad odour. I couldn't pass it for discrimination because I figured it was gracious of her to tell me, very brave too.

Why am I telling such an embarrassing moment to the world, you might ask? I tell this story because of the adolescent girls I love and work with, as well as the women who have a self-esteem story to tell and who need to let go. Self-esteem is your opinion of yourself, which for most of us is defined by what others have said about us from childhood.

High self-esteem is when you have a good opinion of yourself, and low self-esteem is when you have a bad opinion of yourself. When an event like above happens, your self-esteem plummets even further and most struggle to mend the wounds.

Since self-esteem is all about how much we feel valued, loved, accepted, and thought well of by others—and how much we value, love, and accept ourselves—when I was told I smelled, I felt worthless.

This was a poignant point in my life. I could have taken it in many different ways: thinking this was a racial confrontation, thinking that this was the end of my dreams ("Everyone will always think I smell"), or making it into an opportunity to build up my self-esteem and care for myself as suggested by this nice lady.

It was very brave of her to have the courage that she had. I have no doubt in my heart she meant well. This is one of those situations that is difficult no matter how one looks at it. I had an opportunity to host someone from Africa in my home about ten or so years later, and yes, they too had an odour that was very strong, and this time because I was now accustomed to the USA smell (whatever that is) I smelled the difference. I did not say anything.

I just made sure they had soap, lotion, perfumes ready in the bathroom to help them rid of this odour, as I was worried about people would react when they left my home. Until today, I never told them my story or that I detected a strong smell, which made me realize why, in my early years, I had been helped by the lady at National College.

I have had to build up a healthy sense of self-esteem throughout the years, and I am now able to feel good about myself, appreciate my own worth, and take pride in my abilities, skills, and accomplishments.

How did I do it? I finished and graduated High School, my ticket to a better world. I then attended and graduate from Four Universities, attended a lot of conferences, seminars, and grooming classes, pursued my skills and abilities through higher education, and most of all, I did it by working with young adolescents and women.

This situation actually fuelled my ambition to become somebody and to have the independence to smell good and look good when I needed to. I now always make sure that I own only designer perfumes and soaps to never smell bad again. Don't get me wrong; for a moment I thought this situation was definitely an example of discrimination. I was the only black person in the office.

To help me adjust to the USA, my parents sent my sister, 'Star' Sithabile Mahlatini-Kahari, to live with me after I had been at the school for only one quarter, because I missed home so much and cried to them all the time that I couldn't make it. Her arrival meant that I had family here, that I had a partner, and together we could support and encourage each other, which really helped.

The joy was short-lived, as after the first year, Dad was not able to afford the required foreign currency. We had to make another drastic choice, to move from Rapid City,

52
Thriving Beyond the Tears - *Bruised and Never Broken* | Dr. Stem Mahlatini

South Dakota to Boston, Massachusetts, where a friend of mine had told us there were jobs in the nursing homes that paid $8.00 an hour. This was heaven-sent; we could now have the opportunity to work and to pay for our school—so I thought.

I ended up working for a year before I could afford to get back to school. My sister and I stayed with a friend who was gracious enough to take us in when we moved to Boston, and because her home was very small for two more people, we had to take turns sleeping.

Even though there were many challenges associated with this living arrangement, I am choosing to focus on gratitude and to tell you that my sister and I made a decision to work for a year, get our own place, and buy a car together. It turned out to be the best decision we ever made, because it was no easy task living with other people.

When it comes to getting what you want, challenges/problems can be the stepping stones you need to take you to higher ground. This reminds me of the story of the horse who fell into a dry well.

The owner was so devastated as the hole was so deep and difficult for the horse to climb out. The owner and some of his neighbors decided there was no hope and started burying the horse alive. They threw in sand to cover the hall.

However, as they were throwing the sand down the hole, the horse simply went over the sand shook it off his back and kept climbing up until he was rescued. The sand became the horses' stones. Many view problems, challenges as a means to an end, I have seen these changes as stepping stones to who I have become. I believe each trouble is a permanent design that helps get stronger.

I struggle with the high school youths I counsel who demand RESPECT from teachers and adults instead of biting their tongues and striving to gain an education that will earn them eternal respect. I tell them all the time that most of the things they get away with, I would not have attempted with my parents before I was put in my place.

The same applies to employees who choose to butt heads with their superiors instead of earning their respect or gaining the experience that will elevate them to higher paying positions. This should not be taken in the wrong way; I do know that there are some teachers and employers that can benefit from an attitude check from time to time.

However this should not be the child's role to tell off these teachers, I believe that it is even more puzzling to me that there are no consequences in school or home for some of the behaviours I have witnessed.

How did I adjust and finally make it through school? I worked two jobs. I worked 7 a.m.–3 p.m. in the nursing home as a nursing assistant (nurse's aide), went to school from 6 p.m.–9 p.m., then went to work at a residential program from 11 p.m.–6 a.m. so that I would have time to get back to the nursing home. Sleep was a luxury; it was often difficult to stay focused due to the lack of sleep. The thought of the freedom and the opportunity of living independently gave me the confidence to successfully carry this schedule until I graduated with my bachelor's degree.

I paid for my classes, but because I could not afford a full course load, I went part-time for about seven years and obtained my first two degrees, an associate degree in Business Administration and a bachelor's degree in Liberal Arts, that way. This was a bittersweet achievement, because it took me so long and it took a lot out of me to make this happen. The thrill of graduation and the delight of knowing I could be successful later drove me right back into seeking a higher and higher education.

Lessons Learned

The move from Zimbabwe to the USA had a lot of lessons in store for me. I learned that whatever I faced, and whatever circumstances weigh us down, we can always choose the way we respond to them. I have this quote I made for my youth that states:

"It's not what happens to you or who said what to you that matters, it is the way you respond that matters."

How you live your life is totally up to you. It is not dependent upon your circumstances. It is totally dependent on your choices.

In seeking a better life, our outer circumstances might change while our inner conversation might stay the same—especially if we are holding on to ancient, angry, or painful memories.

Our interior life is ours to shape, and, like psychic baggage, it follows us wherever we go. "Sometimes in the winds of change we find our true direction." So, what challenges have you faced? We all face challenges; the key is not in having certain challenges to face, but in how we handle the challenges we do face. I have been a guest speaker at many conferences, and each time I am reminded of how difficult it is to adjust to life in this country, and of how many people continue to struggle to obtain basic needs when they arrive in the USA.

One other lesson for me was to be open to the idea of change, to show a willingness to start afresh despite my background or my origins. I had to take whatever work was available. I lived in the church basement for a while. I accepted hand-me-downs and food from the generous people from the church who helped us; whatever it took.

I never lost sight of where I was going, and that helps. I never lost hope, and I kept dreaming and seeking opportunities here in America, this land of opportunity. I believed God had bigger plans for me. I held onto Jeremiah 29:1,

"For I know the plans I have for you," declares the LORD, "plans to prosper you and not to harm you, plans to give you hope and a future."

No job was too small; no offer of help was demeaning. It all helped me get to where I wanted to go, to get an education; to find work that would pay me substantial money or allow me to run my own business. It is critical to know where you are going, to have a direction.

A Dose of Motivation

Life does not always present us with an ideal situation in which everything works out according to our plans or our wishes. That is where your belief—Thriving Beyond anything you have ever done, the faith and action that will move mountains—comes in.

We must motivate ourselves to do what we must do to get on with our lives. We have to create the life that we want. But first you have to decide what you want in your life. Many of the people I know are working two or three jobs to make ends meet, building homes back in Zimbabwe or maintaining businesses back in Zimbabwe.

My question is, have you decided when and how you will enjoy that home? When will you enjoy the benefits of your business? For those that are just working and not seeing how they can get back to school, start a business, or build back home if that is their desire, I say to you: *It's possible.* You can start by answering the questions below, determining what you want, and making time to get it.

We all have twenty-four hours in the day; it's how you choose to use your twenty-four hours that matters. You do not need money to start pursuing your dream; it helps along the way, but your decision to know where you want to go and what you want is what truly matters. The way will come. Trust in the Lord to do his part and to carry you through. You have to believe that it is possible.

So let's have you start your journey to a life of your own making by answering the following:

1. What do you want in your life?
2. Do you feel worthy of achieving everything you desire?
3. Are there things in your past that have made you feel unworthy?
4. What can you do to encourage yourself, to raise your self-esteem, and to be worthy of the life you wish for?

Thriving Beyond the Tears - *Bruised and Never Broken* | Dr. Stem Mahlatini

3

Education is Power
Lessons Learned

"As long as we are persistent in our pursuit of our deepest destiny, we will continue to grow. We cannot choose the day or time when we will fully bloom. It happens in its own time."

Denis Waitley

61

Chapter 3
Education Is Power
Lessons Learned

Although I think it is very easy to explain the importance of education, it is important to start this chapter by emphasizing another favorite quote on persistence: "Ambition is the path to success. Persistence is the vehicle you arrive in." – Bill Bradley. Persistence is sticking with it despite your circumstances, and that is the key to understanding the importance of education.

Why is education so important, and how do you determine if there is a need to pursue it in your life? Well, when life is not what you expected because you cannot afford to pay your bills, or when you cannot afford to take time off to enjoy a well-earned vacation, or when you cannot easily afford to do what your heart desires due to lack of money, then you will know the importance of education.

For those who are parents, it is the moment when you cannot afford to give your children what they desire or need that makes you realize the importance of education.

I realized really quickly when I arrived in the USA that I needed to focus on obtaining an education in order to better my life. I just knew without any doubt that life would be different if I received some form of training or education.

The minimum-wage jobs I was doing were tedious, difficult, and depressing. The one thing that helped me to focus on going to school was the promise I had made to my parents, my friends, and my family—that is, to seek an education in the United States. I knew that this was the number-one reason I was here, so I had to find ways and means of earning an education.

When I asked around, many of the people I spoke to gave me similar answers which mirror my thoughts on why education is the key to a good life. Education rubs out all the wrong beliefs or misconceptions in our minds. "It helps to create a clear picture of everything around us, and we no longer remain in confusion about the things we learn," said one gentleman I spoke to.

Some people said, "Education brings up questions and also helps us to devise ways to find satisfactory answers to them." "It is about knowing that everything has a science to it, learning to reason about everything until every question meets its answer." "Education can guide us to enlightenment." "It is education that makes it possible for every individual to build the confidence to take decisions, to face life, and to accept successes and failures." This one is my favourite answer; it teaches us to have a sense of pride, one that will sustain us in difficult times.

Deciding to get an education is one thing; getting it is another. I realized that there were many people who wished and wanted to go to school, but who had never found the ways or means of doing it. I was determined to be different and to do what I came here for. This was in the 1980s, and things were different in America; foreigners would take classes and make payment plans, so I am not sure how much is given nowadays to foreign students in the USA.

Let this not deter you, because where there is a will, there is either a way, or excuses for why you can't do something. Nonetheless, nothing was served to me on a silver platter; I had to make my own way. I had taken two quarters' worth of classes at a very small college, National College in Rapid City, South Dakota.

My parents were only able to pay for these two quarters because I had begged them to also send my sister Sithabile (nicknamed Star) to America, and they ended up using monies reserved for my schooling to send my sister to live here with me.

Studies show that no human beings are able to survive properly without education. Education teaches one how to think strategically and creatively, as well as how to work properly and make well-informed decisions, and makes it possible to be a versatile person that can be comfortable in any situation.

I work with high school students, providing them with counseling, life- and career-coaching services. The struggle, I find, is that it is easy for them to blow schoolwork off and perform badly behaviorally and emotionally, even when they have all supports in place to help them. For them and for all adults wishing to go to school, before you pursue your education, ask yourself and answer the following questions.

– *What does education mean to you?*
– *What would you do differently with an education?*

To me, education is power. It is life. Education is not only obtained at colleges; it is found at any place where we can grow spiritually, emotionally, and physically. To me, it is not just classroom work or homework; it is the ability to experience the world through other people's eyes, the opportunity to learn new ways of pursuing your life's dream, the ability to make mistakes and find ways to go on, and it is learning how to take risks and experience life in ways you never would have thought of without education's revelation.

It is the ability to do whatever is necessary to get the life you want. My education has given me a competitive edge in the mental health, speaking, and coaching fields. Attending college classes gave me a sense of pride and renewed my confidence and my spirit.

I know there will be people reading this and saying, "Receiving a college degree is not the world to me, because it will not save me if I'm on my deathbed, it will not buy me love, and it doesn't guarantee me that I won't face challenges in life." There are some who will say or think that they don't really think education is the only way to be successful and to have a productive and fulfilling life. They know a lot of people that have bachelor's degrees or master's degrees and who are not successful or happy with their life.

I say to you, you are correct; however, education will give you the satisfaction of knowing that you are able to achieve whatever you put your mind to. You can have the peace of mind of knowing that you don't have to settle for a minimum-wage job.

You will have peace of mind knowing you can fend for yourself and your children with no stress and without depending on someone to care for you. I do believe, though, that "this piece of paper," as someone called it, will open new opportunities for you if you plan it that way and if you seek new opportunities. It will give you more flexibility if you want to work part-time, or, perhaps, if you wish to work from home and still make good money.

I know the one thing that drove me to do whatever was necessary to get educated is the fact that I like the finer things in life; I am not willing to settle for an average life of just getting by. I love a good life, which is not a minimum-wage-job lifestyle, so for me to get to where I wanted, I needed to pursue the education that would open the doors of opportunity I needed to get me to my dream lifestyle.

I now know that we often limit our own blessings by the way we talk or think about our current situation.

Lessons Learned

We may be highly educated, but if we are without a meaningful combination of thoughts and feelings, a good way to use that education is to get you more money. That way, you can live a stress-free life, pay for what you need, and build the life you have always wanted.

Then again, you might not want to pursue higher education if you have an original idea to help you start creating and to make money to sustain you and your family. So, yes, education is not all. I also believe that not everyone is cut out for higher education—that is, a full four-, six-, or ten-year degree. For some, technical college is sufficient.

My sister, Star Kahari, has a four-year degree and one year of beauty school training. She has long known she wanted to own and operate her own salon, so to her, that one-year certificate would have been sufficient, but I tell you that when it comes to owning her own business, the four years she spent in college have not been in vain.

She has been so good at running her own salon, Kreative Hair Designs in Lynn, Massachusetts, for the last twelve years partly because of the business degree she has. It makes a difference. Persistence and determination are key.

A Dose of Motivation

Every goal that has ever been reached began with just one step and the belief that the goal could be attained. Dreams really do come true, but the results usually come because of hard work, determination, and persistence.

Look deep within your heart and determine what would better your life. Think about what you desire, and find the strength to work at pursuing your passion. You will find strength within you that you never knew you had. Education is key; it is life.

The following will help jump-start you:

- Attend church seminars, life coaching seminars, continuing education, and professional development training sessions.

- Don't let old mistakes or misfortunes hold you back. Learn from them, forgive yourself and forgive others, and move on. Only you can do this. Choose to take control of your life.

- Learn something new every day, by reading a new book or by watching or listening to something motivational or inspiring.

- The answer is within you. Learn from others. Be interested in what they know and in how they can help you.

- It is your sweat, your frustrations, and your hard work that will bring you the life you seek.

Thriving Beyond the Tears - *Bruised and Never Broken* | Dr. Stem Mahlatini

4

The Power of Believing in Yourself and Your Dreams

"A successful person is one who can lay a firm foundation with the bricks that others throw at him or her." David Brinkley

Thriving Beyond the Tears - *Bruised and Never Broken* | Dr. Stem Mahlatini

Chapter 4
The Power of Believing in Yourself and Your Dreams

G rowing up, I was privileged to meet a lot of people who had the chance to leave Zimbabwe and go to other countries to seek a better life. There was a significant difference between those who came back with their lives reflecting a major change and those who came back but their lives were the same.

The difference, I think, had to do with attitude, ambition, having dreams to pursue, and having the ability to endure hardship. I came to the United States believing that life would be better, so no matter how difficult it got (or how difficult it gets), I held onto the belief that my life could and would get better.

From the time I was in primary school at the Kurai and Wadzanai primary schools, I was a hard worker. Despite the poverty—walking to school with no shoes, wearing slippers from Bata when times were good, getting rained on during bad weather—I was determined to believe my life could and would be better.

I had no doubt that God had bigger plans for me and my family than the struggles we faced. I have been a prayer warrior from a very young age, when I attended the Anglican Church in Section 3 of Kambuzuma Township.

I was a faithful member who believed, and who still believes, that God keeps his promises, that he never forgets, and that he will remember me in my prayers. I believed those things because of my faith. I didn't realize at that time that I was planting a seed in my heart of wanting to do better, preparing fertile ground for a fighting spirit that would help me to survive in the United States.

I believe that God, the Creator, Allah, or whomever you believe to be your creator, created us all to lead a good life—a successful, stress-free life. I believe that before we were born, he laid out a plan for each of us, and in this plan our path is laid out with each moment we will face in our life.

The people we will meet, the places we will go, the work we will do, the families we will have, the misfortunes we will face, the pain, the difficult moments, the favors we will encounter—all of these things are laid out.

I believe this life outline is destined to happen, no matter how good, bad, educated, uneducated, rich or poor we are. The major importance of this is that we must encounter difficulties in our lives, but what matters is how we deal with each phase and each moment.

When I started work as a nurse's aide in the nursing home, it was such a demeaning and gross job that I would never have pictured myself doing it in a million years. Many people were working in the nursing home when I first came there in the early 80s, and they spoke so badly about what we were doing ... and yet, they kept doing the work.

I landed this job as a favor of the Lord; it lifted me up from the church basement and brought me to higher ground. At first, I was elated to get the paycheck and not interested in the job itself. It was just a way to make ends meet and to pay for my tuition.

It wasn't until I sat down and determined where I was going, why I was here, and what I wanted in life, that this very dirty job became a blessing, and so did the patients I served. I realized that these were real people, like me, who had aged, or who were disabled and therefore unable to care for themselves.

Thriving Beyond the Tears - *Bruised and Never Broken* | Dr. Stem Mahlatini

They relied on me to care for them; they relied on me to feed, change and bathe them, and to be there in their private moments because they had no choice. It was then that I prayed for the patience to care for them and for the strength to do the work without complaining, without grumbling, and without becoming angry.

I prayed, and I conquered. The more I accepted where I was, knowing that this very job would elevate me to where I wanted to go, opportunities opened for me, people were more helpful, and I found myself being blessed Thriving Beyond measure.

My blessings—and they were blessings, though you might never have believed it—were having patients that had not spoken say "Thank you" or just say "Hello." I was so happy to hear from them, and I was glad when they smiled because I knew that was their way of saying "Thank you."

I felt obligated to do my best as the person God had chosen to care for his children on his behalf. When I looked at my work and my life from a biblical perspective, taking the view that God has control of my life and all that will happen to me, I felt a sense of relief like no other. I remembered what my mother always says to me—that when you do something from your heart, people are grateful, and their gratitude or "Thank you" is a prayer for you. I have always believed that, and even today, when someone is grateful for my work, I rejoice because I know those blessings will come back to me one day.

I say all this to remind you that sometimes we have no idea what it is we are supposed to do with our lives, so we should be open and do good at all times. Then, the true you will be revealed. That gratitude you receive is a prayer for your future, for your life.

One good thing is that it is never too late to start doing good, to start living from the heart, to start dreaming, to start serving others and doing what you do from the heart, as well as loving from the heart. The key is to believe in what makes you feel good and what makes you feel happy—to believe that your willingness to take risks, to take opportunities that come your way, and to work hard towards getting what you want, will bring you the rewards you deserve.

When you find yourself becoming discouraged with some part of your current personal or professional life, ask yourself what you believe in. Life will give you what you ask of it, what you believe you deserve; the key is to wholeheartedly pursue your life's goals with an open mind, believing that you can change your life at any moment. Your hard work will be rewarded. How do I know? Because I have studied, read about, and met people like you and me who have done well in life only because they had a dream, they believed, and they worked hard.

Many people whom I have coached and advised have said to me that it is easier for some, because some people have not had a past like theirs. Yes, some have had a past that was difficult, a past full of painful memories of sexual, physical, and emotional abuse. It is difficult to cope with this past. It requires a lot of effort to work through the pain, but the good news is that it is possible to overcome these memories and to live a purposeful life.

The important thing to remember is you have to make up your mind to work at ridding yourself of these defeating emotions, feelings, and memories. I have had people come to me and ask for us to pray for openness before we start therapy, because they feel they might sabotage their own healing. So, whatever it takes, commit yourself to defeating the inner pains that have prevented you from believing and dreaming.

Lessons Learned

It is very important—I mean very important—to have an idea of what you desire in life, of what your dream is. It is important to create and pursue a dream, no matter your age, because as long as we are alive, we can dream, we can believe, and we can pursue our dream.

I have heard before that if you imagine yourself on top of a mountain, you can choose to wing your way toward the clouds, or you can simply walk the usual, ordinary paths that lead to the valley below. I now know that the sky is not a limit; there are no limits. We can do whatever we want to do, be whoever we want to be, as long as we believe and act diligently toward achieving what we want.

There will, no doubt, be difficult times ahead; there will be situations that will take you away from doing what you want to do. You will face illness, marriage problems, challenges with raising children, financial challenges, infertility, lack of love, drug or alcohol use, jail time, eviction. These things happen; they all can happen to the best of us.

They may at times seem too great to handle, and doubt and fear will strengthen your belief that it is too much to face, but your faith, and the knowledge that others have overcome these challenges, will pull you through.

A Dose of Motivation

It is the courage, the belief, the determination, the willingness to face challenges and the willingness to take chances that will ease your life, give you what you want, and better your situation.

It's not about having everything going right at all times; it is about facing whatever goes wrong with the faith that this, too, shall pass. It's about having the determination to go on in spite of the obstacles in your way, to serve time if you have to, to go through life's storms when faced with them—because there will be a time when all is well and the storms finally pass by.

Know that you are bigger than the moment, however terrible it is; you have everything within you to deal with any situation that comes your way, and when it seems too much to handle, surrender to a higher power and be still. It's not where you stand or where your life is at the moment that is important; it is where you are going that truly matters. That is why it is critical to determine where you are going.

My mother's tears and prayers helped me set sail. I created my dream life when I heard mother praying. She said, "Lord, let my pain, suffering and tears be a blessing to my children." My path has been ordained and blessed, but it was, and is, up to me to work at getting all that she prayed for. I believe with all my heart that God heard those prayers and will reward all of us children for those times mother cried out to God. I believe God is not done blessing us yet.

The questions you should ask yourself are:

(a) What do you believe in?
(b) What dreams and wishes for your life do you have?

Your path, too, has been prayed for, as I have yet to see any mother who does not pray for her children. All mothers openly or secretly pray for their children, so your path has been prayed for, too. Believe and trust that your life will get better, that it can get better—because it's true.

It's not about understanding why something happened. Why someone would do what they did. It's about rising above all that happened. It's about being able to believe in your heart of hearts that there will always be more good than bad in this world.

There are and there will be good, trustworthy people around you. Remember, we only have today, and tomorrow is not promised to any of us; however, if we live to the best of our ability, tomorrow will bring new, exciting opportunities.

This is your life—take the power to choose what you will do with it. Choose to dream big, do big, and love big. You, and only you, can control your happiness and your achievements in life. Make it a worthwhile journey

5

Dealing With Fear
And Failure

"The Key to Change ... is to let go of fear."

Rosanne Cash.

Thriving Beyond the Tears - *Bruised and Never Broken* | Dr. Stem Mahlatini

Chapter 5
Dealing With Fear And Failure

Fear and failure are two words that I know well; they were my daily bread for me when I was growing up. I was always afraid of doing badly and failing, because the expectations associated with being the firstborn were very high. I heard so often that I was a leader and needed to be an example to my siblings, my family, and my community.

In Zimbabwe, families are very close, so it is not surprising to have people who you do not know telling you to stop doing something or just watching your every move. Every adult has the right to watch over you, give you advice, and most of all, report to your parents any behaviors they see as bad. Hence I always feared disappointing all of the people who believed in me even before I believed in myself—those who, in one form or another, helped to shape the person who I have become.

In primary and secondary school, I put a great deal of effort into attending classes, studying for exams, and making sure I behaved well. I always received C's, so at times I honestly couldn't see myself getting far, because the studying I had done did not help to improve my grades. I knew, however, that quitting was not an option. It became critically important to deal with my own fears from a very early age, and I relied on inspiration and motivation, which came through many channels.

I went to church diligently, with no excuses, to hear what the Lord had planned for me. I spoke to people who were uplifting. I read books. I was curious—very curious, as my parents would tell me. I am sure many who are reading this book will remember the poem "Don't Quit." I used this poem to inspire me whenever I faced discouragement, when I felt afraid, and when I didn't believe in myself.

Here is a reminder. It goes like this:

DON'T QUIT
As every one of us sometimes learns,
And many a failure turns about
When you might have won had you stuck it out;
Don't give up though the pace seems slow,
You may succeed with another blow.
Success is failure turned inside out—
The silver tint of the clouds of doubt,

And you never can tell how close you are,
It may be near when it seems so far;
So stick to the fight when you're hardest hit—
It's when things seem worst that you mustn't quit.
— Author Unknown

I now use this same poem to motivate, uplift and inspire others, hoping that many will take it to heart and believe that they have what it takes to make the best of their lives. My motto has long been, "Quitting is not an option." I actually really believe, from the bottom of my heart, and that is why, before throwing in the towel, I give all opportunities a fair chance.

To quit would be a frightening excuse to let a growing talent languish within me. To quit is to give in to the opposition—to give in to those people who thought and who said that I would amount to nothing. To quit is one way of agreeing with that inner voice within me, the one that expresses fear and tells me how incapable I am.

Among the failures I have encountered, one in particular comes to mind. It happened when I was blessed with a very high-paying job (at least, it was considered high paying at that time) in Tampa, Florida. I was being paid $18,000 as a master's level social worker, and I felt so depressed, deprived, and underpaid. I decided to do what many today still doubt: paid a tithe and prayed for God's guidance.

I was tired of complaining and of nothing changing. I knew that with my master's degree and my experience, I could do more and earn more. I gave my whole paycheck of $950.00, representing two weeks of work, as a commitment to my savior and to show that I was ready for change.

It took a week for me to see my blessing, but I saw it when I attended training in Tampa at the local University. There was a lady in the training class who came to me during the break and asked if I was licensed as a Social Worker. I said "Yes," and she said, "If you want a job in Tampa, let me know. We are looking for licensed people."

I could not believe my ears. The job paid $52,000 US dollars a year, a fortune in comparison to my previous salary. I was sold. Needless to say, I got the job and moved from Orlando to Tampa. For those in doubt, tithing and offerings work; they do.

I worked there for a year with no problems, and then came the unexpected failure. I had my annual evaluation, and out of nowhere my supervisor said I was not doing the work according to their policies. She noted numerous things I had done wrong, which was a shock to me, as no one had pointed to me that I was doing anything wrong. I had applied for a promotion and she said I was not eligible; actually, she wrote me up, giving me a warning right at that moment.

I was shocked; I felt numb and helpless. Within two weeks I was fired. I was stunned; I was devastated. How could I have failed at this high-paying job? I remember my embarrassment as I drove from this job, playing the song by Donnie McClurkin, "Stand," which said when a situation like this presented to you and I God says you can make it , will you still stand and trust me. With tears in my eyes I found myself saying "Yes Lord, I will Trust you.

To me, this was God's voice telling me to just stand; he was telling me that he has a purpose for my life and that he needed to move me. I truly was not thinking of moving. I was very content, even though the job was so stressful and challenging.

After three months of fasting, praying, and doing menial jobs, I got the job of a lifetime as a Transplant Social Worker with Tampa General Hospital. I loved this job, as I saw God's hand at work first-hand, whether it was in the operating room, in the boardroom where the decisions to do a transplant or not were made, or with the families who waited patiently for loved ones to heal.

I was instrumental; I felt God's hand in all that I did, and I found myself confidently pursuing my doctorate studies with no hassle. I needed to be moved. It was not a failure, after all. Six months after I was fired, one girl from that company called me and told me they had been all let go. The company went out of business. There were over sixty licensed social workers looking for work, and the Lord had moved me and given me a job before everyone else was let go. What a lesson in failure and faith! His plans are better than I could ever imagine.

I have had my share of many other instances I call failures, and it is interesting that what comes to mind next is marriage. I have been married before for a very short period. I was with Harold Marks, a gentle, loving, and kind man, who tried his level best. I will forever respect him.

We dated for ten years and married for less than a year before we divorced. Why did this happen, I ask myself? Looking back, I dated him for ten years however we had differences that made me think we were not meant for each other. Like many people, I ignored the voice and the feelings that kept nagging within me that this was not to be. We broke up many times during the ten years we dated.

I knew that we were having difficulties and he knew it, but we hung in there. It was easy for me to hang in there because I was in school doing my doctorate studies, and I was so busy that I totally paid a blind eye to my relationship. I didn't want to work on it, or break it off.

I was content just having him around when he could be. Thinking about it, this was not only a failure on my part, but the fear of being alone also played a big part in my staying with him for so long. What I know now is that when you are in that state of fear, you give yourself so many reasons to explain why it is hard to do something. I now realize these are all excuses. The funny thing is, when you say the reasons, more often than not you end up truly believing you are right, and that it's truly not possible.

I know I am not alone in the quest to start a family, or in wishing to fall in love, get married and start a family. Like most ladies in my age group, forty to fifty years of age, who are not married and don't have kids, I chose pursuing an education over marriage. I truly listened to what my parents wanted for me to do, which was to be educated. I placed more focus on that than on starting a family. I have beat myself up about what I could have done, why I just didn't get married, then go to school, why this, why that, and I find myself more afraid of not knowing the answers than of just being.

And yes it's true the more education expertise you hold, the more intimidating you are to most men. I have no doubt that the right man will not be intimidated, as he will see the true me and not my degrees and profession. It's amazing how you work so hard to be somebody and at the end of it all you still yearn to have a family and find yourself struggling to find the right person.

I have Hope, that soon I will have a testimony to write in my next book about how my blessing finally came to pass, so let's keep praying and being still. I also strongly believe that my life is ordered, as I have mentioned previously. If I were to be married and have children, it could have happened despite my ambitions.

I believe, and strongly believe, that God has not forgotten me. I believe he knows my heart. He knows my wishes and my dreams of falling in love and marrying someone who will love me unconditionally until the end. I am content with my life.

At forty-seven, I am content with God's plans. I am hesitant to say that if having kids is not in God's plan then I am ok with the plan, because I still believe that miracles can happen. I will have kids and be married. It is my prayer that the unforeseen will happen to me. To be married and have children at forty-seven will be a testimony I will live to tell.

My goal and my lifelong dream is to be an instrument of Hope and of Peace to those I serve. I enjoy talking to people. I take pleasure in making them feel good and in contributing to their understanding of themselves, their situations, and their past. Working with adolescents and women has allowed me the opportunity to know that one can make an impact despite one's fears.

I love seeing the happiness and the pride in the high school students I work with when they finally get it and start working hard at obtaining their high school diplomas. Many have not seen their future, but they build up their dreams to help them stay on course, and they work hard to get the key to their future: the high school diploma.

I believe I am a vessel and I pray that I will be made into more than an ordinary servant. My goal is to continue to ignite the inner strength that we all possess to create the life that we want. To motivate and inspire others to greatness is my goal and my heart, so I am open to any and all lessons as I move along my life path. We all have one life to live, so letting fear, anger or resentment keep us stuck could easily be seen as a waste of one's precious life.

I believe my life story will be a boost of confidence to those who await their right partner and family. My faith and my knowledge of God's supernatural powers have sustained me. I believe that with God, all things are possible. I have faith that because I have waited, my strength will be renewed and I will see the impossible happening.

The most difficult challenge with me being a public figure is that everyone has high expectations of me; they celebrate each time I date, and when it fails, I am left to deal with the rejection and failure in public. I have learned to be still and wait. I have learned to be content with what people will say about my status as a single person with no kids of my own. I have learned to be secretive and not say who I am dating before he is The One; that is part of being still and knowing that all things will work together for his greatness.

The pain and stress of being alone and childless have in some ways led to a journey of self-discovery. I have been to see therapists to talk about my emotions, I have been prayed for, I have taught and participated in training sessions that focus on the pain and the stress of being single and childless. I have even preached on the topic of being single.

Through all this, I have seen myself coping with the fear of being alone, the fear of not being a mother, and the fear of failing in my marriage in a much better way. I also know that for me to testify about this lone journey is to give empowerment and inspiration to many who are going through the same struggles.

It is okay not to be married, it is okay not to have children of my own, and it is okay to believe until it is impossible. In my case, I have no doubt my children will be a testimony to God's mercies and to the power of prayer and belief.

I have no doubt that my tears and the struggles I have endured as I yearn for true love and a family will be a blessing to many who will read my books, attend my seminars, or listen to my radio and television shows. I have no doubt. I remain expectant. I humbly wait.

All of us dream of doing well in our lives; we all want to be successful. All of us have big dreams, even though at times some people think they do not dream. There is a fire within each of us, a desire to be someone.

We all try very hard to achieve our goals, our dreams; we do. But on our journey to achieving those dreams, if we face a failure, a stumbling block, we might just break down completely. Sometimes, for some, it becomes difficult to keep trying to get something because of the failures they faced before.

What ends up happening is that even when you try to work on achieving something, when you have this feeling of defeat, you are not able to put 100% into pursuing what you want. You feel discouraged, and as a result, you find excuses to avoid the issue and stop working towards what you want. Intentionally or unintentionally, the fear of failure affects all of our efforts or our performances at one time or another.

One of my goals was to be a publisher, a motivational/inspirational speaker, and a trainer/coach. I was never afraid of being in front of people; however, I was afraid of my accent, afraid that people would not understand me. I was afraid of what people would say. I was afraid of being a failure.

This fear brought with it stage fright, which I had never before had. When I met my friend, Dr. John Loblack from Tampa, Florida, it was as if he knew my heart. We clicked because his ambition is also focused on speaking, coaching and training. He, however, was way ahead of me in preparation, so he started sharing books, tapes, seminars he had attended and organizations he had joined to master his speaking and coaching.

I became a student of speaking by listening to the late Jim Rohn, Dennis Whitley, Les Brown, Zig Ziggler, Louise Hay, Dr. Wayne Dyer, and many others. I joined the Rotary Club, Toastmasters and the National Speakers Association (NSA). To get rid of my stage fright, I started volunteering to speak at churches, company meetings, retreats, Toastmasters, and Rotary Clubs as a volunteer.

I like the saying that says, "To conquer fear, you just have to do what you are afraid of." The experience I gained, coupled with my dream to inspire and motivate others, continues to help me in my career today.

To gain the experience and confidence I need will require continued exposure and action on my part, as I continue my journey of persuading others that they have within them the ability and the powers they need to change their life and to live the life they desire. I believe we all have

God-given and fantastic powers within us, powers that, when fearlessly released, will make us into extraordinary people.

I will never forget a beautiful card I received from my first life career coach, Sasha ZeBryk, who is an author, speaker, and executive speech coach. It said, "Many of our fears are tissue-paper thin, and a single courageous step would carry us clear through them. ~Brendan Francis."

I knew then that I had nothing to fear, and I went headfirst into my speaking and coaching business. I have never looked back. Fear is indeed tissue-paper thin. I cannot emphasize enough the benefits of having a life career coach that can help you along the way; it is truly a priceless investment.

Coming from Zimbabwe, I was at first very skeptical about self-investment or personal development, because I felt that it was money I could use to pay bills or to send home. I realized, however, after several encounters with mentors, colleagues, and people who have made it in their lives, that personal development and self-investment are key.

I learned to care for myself and to gain experience related to how I will help others overcome the things I have had to overcome, with fear being the number-one issue that got in my way.

Lessons Learned

The first lesson is to stop looking at failure in a negative way or as a negative thing. Most people tend to associate failure with weakness, stupidity, and dumbness. I totally disagree with that. I believe and I know that if you are doing something, and you think you are just perfect in it, that means something seriously is going wrong with it.

When one thinks he or she is perfect, then that means that they have closed all doors that might lead to growth or improvement. I have learned the hard way that whenever there is a failure, there are a million chances for improvement. Failures and fears have made me more determined to empower pursue their dreams despite of their fears.

I travel around the world as a Susan Jeffers–certified "Feel the Fear and Do It Anyway" Coach, Speaker and Trainer in order to speak to many about fear. It is apparent that we should look at failure as simply another step toward success, and also as a step toward opportunities to change and grow. Strive to make yourself positive enough to see the good side of failure at all times.

The second lesson is refraining from labeling yourself a 'failure.' It won't help, and may actually discourage you from trying again. But if you don't try again, you won't succeed. So think of it as having found a way that doesn't work; now you just need to try something else.

The third lesson is not to try to frustrate yourself by whacking at the problem in the same way again and again like a machine that only has one function. Try a different approach; you might be amazed at the results you get when you attack the problem in a new way or by looking at it from a new angle.

The fourth lesson: Be patient. Rome was not built in a day. Many small steps forward will get you to your end goal, even if each step seems insignificant.
For my Christian believers out there, the following are lessons and beliefs that have helped me cope with my fears in a more mature, Christian way.

(1) Strongly believe that a Christian can become successful in spite of past failures because of God's incredible grace and forgiveness. We may have to live

with the results of some of our failures or sins, yet God is free to continue to love us in Christ and use us for His purposes because of grace (John 21 & Peter).

(2) Seek to use failures as lessons for promoting growth and change.

(a) Understand that failures remind us of the consequences of our decisions. We reap what we sow. This is the law of the harvest. Failures remind us of what can happen. They can make us careful, but they should not be allowed to paralyze us.

(b) After recognizing that our failures show us what we should and should not do, they become lessons in where we went wrong, and why. You know what they say: "Hindsight is 20/20." If we will learn from history, from our past mistakes, it can help us avoid making the same mistake twice.

(3) After failing at something:
- Acknowledge your failures, and refuse to hide behind some lame excuse.
- Confess any sins to God when sin is involved in the failure.
- Study or examine what happened so that you can learn from the failure.

- Put it behind you and move ahead (1 John 1:9 & Phil 3:13).
- Be assured of God's forgiveness; you are forgiven.
- Count on and rest in His forgiveness, and refuse to use the failure as an excuse for morbid introspection, pessimism, self-pity, depression, or fear of moving on; if not for yourself, then for the Lord. Ask Him for forgiveness and move on despite the embarrassment or the fear of ridicule that you might feel.

(4) Choose to grow through failure.
- God loves you despite your faults. His love is unconditional.
- Know that we are not now perfect, nor will we ever be.
- Remember that God still has a plan for our lives. God is not through with us yet, and we need to get on with His plan.

There are many causes of failure.

Yes, there are many causes of failure. Some are the product of specific acts of sin, but some are not. Some are simply the product of ignorance or of circumstances Thriving Beyond our control.

Whether caused by sin or by the many things that can happen Thriving Beyond our control, all failure teaches us the important truth of just how desperately we need God, or a Higher Power, and how much we need his mercy and his grace in our lives. Sometimes our failures are mirrors for criticism, but they can always become tools for growth and for deeper levels of trust and commitment to God if we will respond to them as such, rather than choosing to rebel or become hardened as a result of the difficulty.

As Erwin W. Lutzer put it, "God is adequate for all kinds of failure. Some failures may not be our fault, but they serve as reminders that we must live with eternal priorities in mind. Other failures are directly the result of our own sinful choices."

Regardless, God has made more than adequate provision for us to live a life of freedom and productivity, a life of abundance and peace, in spite of it all.

A Dose of Motivation

Our faithfulness in the present will reap great rewards in the future. When I teach on subjects such as 'living your dream life;' 'overcoming life's obstacles;' 'profits are better than wages;' 'feel the fear and do it anyway;' or 'forgiveness is key to your freedom,' I always emphasize the importance of sticking to your goals and sacrificing for what you want.

As I talk about the sacrifices that must be made, I usually get some discontented stares. But I always leave the attendees with this one question: "How badly do you want it?" Well, how badly?

That's my question to you today.

- Do you want your dream bad enough that you're willing to burn the midnight oil?
- Do you want your dream bad enough to feel the fear and do it anyway?
- Do you want your dream bad enough to withstand criticism and opposition?
- Will you continue to persist in the face of rejection or loss?
- Will you throw in the towel when things do not go as you expected them to?

Make no mistake about it, your confidence and your determination will be tested as you pursue your passions and dreams. But understand that the challenges you will face are not uncommon. As you study the lives of great men and women in history, as well as in contemporary society, let their lives serve as an inspiration that will sustain you through the difficult times. If they made it, in spite of what they had to endure, so can you.

I want to encourage you not to give up just because it's hard. Keep pressing forward. Just know that some of the greatest achievements have their origin in the most complicated and challenging problems. I have learned that where there is great difficulty, there is also great opportunity.

If you've given up on your dream or placed it on the back burner due to difficulties or distractions—moving from your home country, getting married, or having children—I want to challenge you to pick it up again. Reignite your passion and make the decision that you're going to see it through to the end.

Don't make any excuses—just do it! Retaining or hiring a coach will be beneficial in getting started, if you are hesitant or unsure. "Success seems to be connected with action. Successful men keep moving. They make mistakes, but they don't quit." – Conrad Hilton

Thriving Beyond the Tears - *Bruised and Never Broken* | Dr. Stem Mahlatini

6

Angels Along The Way

"When we forgive evil we do not excuse it, we do not tolerate it, we do not smother it. We look the evil full in the face, call it what it is, let its horror shock and stun and enrage us, and only then do we forgive it." Lewis B. Smedes – Forgive & Forget: Healing the Hurts We Don't Deserve

Thriving Beyond the Tears - *Bruised and Never Broken* | Dr. Stem Mahlatini

Chapter 6
Angels Along The Way

Della Reese is one my favourite ministers and actresses, the one who was the lead angel in "Touched by An Angel." Her delightful interpretation of her life and the people in it (her angels along the way, she called them) was a rude awakening for me.

Her gratefulness and willingness to forgive all of the people in her life, including those who weren't so wonderful to her, put a healthy but confusing perspective back into my life. I say confusing because my mother, my siblings, and I have worked ourselves endlessly to find ways to forgive my father for his heartless way of treating my mother. I know there are many who have bumped heads with me when it comes to my father, because I have been angry, hurt, and confused for many years.

Many reading this memoir have dated him, or known someone he dated, or have hurt my mother in one way or another by being with her husband. I forgive you. I have had many encounters where I have expressed utter disappointment and distress over my father's behavior only because I have witnessed the pain my mother has endured. No woman should ever tolerate such pain for the sake of love.

This book is one way to make it okay for women like my mother to finally talk about the hidden pain of being a wife to a polygamist who has no regard for her heart or her feelings except for the need to have total control. My father, for some reason, has in many ways treated mother like she is a piece of nothing in front of us children. He has demeaned her, ridiculed her, and falsely accused her of cheating, physically and emotionally abusing her Thriving Beyond measure.

My siblings and I have seen and nursed her after she has been brutally beaten or emotionally abused or both. I have many times asked the question, "How do you forgive in such instances?" just as many of you will after reading this. Before I answer that, let me further publicly vent so that you, too, can feel free to finally let it all out and free your hearts.

Mother tells me my father and his second wife stayed in her home, where she endured severe physical abuse for nine years. Why? Why did she let it go for so long? Why was she not strong enough to say "No," to leave, to come to her children for help?

These are the questions every polygamist's children ask. These are the questions the wives of polygamy ask. They wonder why they could not break the cycle. Well, we are breaking the cycle. Polygamy is supposedly a celebrated practice that was done to expand the family—to strengthen the family unit, as I am told.

Mother says that even though it hurts to have another woman with your man, it is believed that if it is done in a manner where you still feel loved, cared for, and respected, you can learn to live with it.

My family is my world. All who know us have always admired us, sneered at us, or jeered at us, but I do not think anyone had or has any idea of what lies behind those smiles, those laughs and those doors.

Revealing the family secrets is taboo in my culture, but what I have learned is that it is difficult to move on in life when your heart is heavy and hurting. I am ready to share my innermost pain in the hope that as I am freed, as my mother is freed, many women, men and children will also be freed from this inner turmoil.

I guess my pain has come from wanting to understand how my father, once a loving, caring man before he became a polygamist, could be so cruel and heartless to my mother—a woman who has stuck by his side for forty-seven years, taken care of his seven children, and kept the Mahlatini name going.

I also struggle with understanding why mother has not let go of my father, why she has not left him mentally or emotionally. I understand it takes two, so she also has a responsibility to stop the mental and spiritual torture that my father's actions have caused.

I can only attribute this to fear—fear of leaving the children to grow up with an uncaring step-mother, or fear of being ridiculed if she went back to her hometown. But mostly, she tells me, it is because her mother told her that no matter what happened in the marriage, she should not leave her children with another woman to raise.

In addition, the inner pain, which I will explain later, can be so crippling that one is unable to make any changes. For that unconditional love and sacrifice, mother, we your seven children— Sithembile, Sithabile, Sidumile, Sibusisiwe, and Simon, are forever grateful.

It is stories and memories—like when mother nearly went blind in 2009 due to stress and inner pain—that most women in Zimbabwe, from the time I left home, had not heard or learned about. Mother's inner pain and stress is not uncommon. Many women in polygamist relationship have learned to suppress their feelings and cater to their husbands and children's needs.

Many are committed for life as they don't feel they have the right or the strength to leave their children and divorce. Mother tells us many times she prayed and asked the Lord to take her especially when she was beaten until she was all swollen and bruised for no apparent reason. My oldest brother witnessed an incident he says still makes him very upset.

He states he went home one afternoon to find mother all swollen and crying after Dad had hit her. Mother begged my brother not to confront my father, saying he needed to keep the respect of father and son so he should leave it alone. He did and it still bothers him how someone could think of hitting our petite mother who is so fragile and vulnerable.

Needless to say after the blindness started getting worse, I rushed home to Zimbabwe to bring mother back to the

USA for treatment. At this time my father had been gone with his second and third wives for over twenty years and had started new families with them. He never bothered to call or to come visit her during the time she was going blind. He however is considered and still is the head of my mother's home even though he has not spend a night in over twenty years and visited only a handful of times.

When father moved out of the house, mother said she refused to leave as he had wanted her to do because that is the house where she had raised us. Another reason was that the home in Waterfalls, Zimbabwe is the only place we all call home; we have nowhere else to go when we visit. He never thinks of how much more mental damage this will cause us the children, his grandchildren let alone my mother.

In the years since, mother has made repairs and kept the house maintained so that when we all visit Zimbabwe we have a place to go. I have been home four times now and it has been a blast being home.

Mother has always beloved that the house was in both their names, entrusting her husband, my father, to have purchased the home in both their names. As the Lord would see it, when my father left the house and decided to move out with his second wife, my mother had to struggle to catch up with the house payments. My sisters, brothers and I had to help pay for the home and we had our mother keep the title deeds after paying the home off.

No one bothered to ask mother to check whose name was on the title deeds. We all relaxed, and believing that this was Mom and Dad's home, and Mom believed it, too. It was not until she had been here in the USA for a year receiving medical treatment that my father called me and said he was selling our home in Waterfalls because he needed the money, moreover mother was now an American.

Moreover, he said, mother was now a US citizen so she didn't need the home anymore. I explained to him that she was only here on a green card and not as a citizen, so she would be coming back home to Zimbabwe after she regained her health. He was so angry and stern, and said he was selling the home anyway, because it was his home. I know many are probably asking why mother got a green card and Dad didn't. Here is the funny synopsis of what happened.

As a firstborn, I knew at some point we would all need to help care for our stepsiblings from the other two mothers.

This revelation came after I completed my doctorate in Florida, moved back to Massachusetts, and realized I was ready to set my life in order.

The biggest aspect of setting my life in order was that I needed to free my mind, and I needed to deal with the deep inner pains caused by my father's decision to practice polygamy. I also knew that his children were innocent, and they would need all the help they could get. I spoke to my six siblings and we all agreed to pay for both Mom and Dad's USA green card applications.

We sent in the applications, and when they were called in for interviews, my father reportedly sat there and told the USA embassy officer that he was not accepting their green card unless his two other wives and their children were also given the green cards necessary in order for them to go to America with him. I am sure the lady looked at him in amazement, as this practice is not lawful or acceptable in the USA.

When she told my father that he could not get green cards for his other wives, he told the officer that the United States could keep their green card, because they have to acknowledge that he is a polygamist and he cannot leave his other families behind.

The embassy gave him a week to think about it and called my brother to tell him the outcome of the interview. I called my father only to be told that my siblings and I had not included his other family members in the application because we wanted to separate them, which was untrue.

I explained to him that what we had actually wanted was for him to get his papers first. Then he could file for his other kids, and that way they in turn could file for their prospective mothers, as we were now doing for him and for our mother. For some reason he was stuck on the idea that the USA didn't or wouldn't understand that he was a polygamist, and he decided that the green card would not split him from his other families.

He declined the card and the application was closed. Mother received her green card and can now travel back and forth between Zimbabwe and the USA without the hassle of applying for a visa. My dad can and will continue to vis

it us; however, he has to apply for a US visa each time. I have no doubt that he will get the visa each time, because they know he is a polygamist who has no intention of staying in the USA—or does he? I may never know.

As far as I know and believe, we did our part. Today I carry no guilt for not having any intention of helping the siblings who were born in the 'small houses,' as they are called in Zimbabwe.

My intentions, together with those of my siblings, were to give them the freedom of living in the USA that we never had growing up. If my father had accepted his green card, which is a temporary visa, he could have filed for all of them, and with those temporary visas they could have travelled to the USA and applied for American tuition assistance programs, advantages we never had. We have had to sweat to reach our goals.

Our success and our education have not come easy. We have had to work very hard to attain everything we have achieved, following a long, tedious, but very rewarding road. To God be the glory for all that we have achieved and continue to attain.

Months later, my father realized that he had missed a great opportunity. I think that at this point he had consulted with some intelligent individuals who had informed him of the right way to handle the green card issue, instead of misleading him accidentally as the close confidants he had relied on the first time had done. It was, however, too late. The file was closed. He called and asked us to try and reopen the case, but to no avail. It was too late. He, however, took it as an indication that we did not want him here, and yet he himself had, unfortunately, declined the opportunity of a lifetime.

Many people wish they could have a chance of getting a green card, as many people find that getting one is a very challenging and difficult process. His reaction was to find ways in which he could be vindictive to us and to our mother, though for what reason, I will never know. He decided that he was going to se

ll the only place we called home—our house in Waterfalls. As I write this section, my heart is heavy, for I recall my mother's tears and pain when I told her the house was being sold. She lost so much weight in only a few days, and I didn't know how to console her. My siblings and I had to hire a lawyer to help us stop him, and that is when, to our amazement, we were told that mother's name was never in the title deeds; the house was only in his name.

We were able to have the lawyers sue my father to stop him from selling the house before mother could go home. Fortunately, many of the people who went to view the home asked about the reasons it was being sold, and upon hearing of the tension between my parents regarding this sale, they decided to refrain from buying the house. Today, we value life more than property, we value health more than property, and we value the grace of God in our lives more than property.

This is the part of the practice of polygamy that I didn't understand, at least at first. As I mentioned before, I wondered for a long time why my mother and many of the other women who have been emotionally and physically abused by their husbands have not left or sought help. I now know, and I wish to share the answer with all those who will read this book.

My hope and my prayer is that this will open a way for many to begin healing. The reason it is so difficult to leave has to do with the inner pain one endures and the inner fears one has of what could happen. For my mother, the pain and the fear of what would happen after she left are the things that kept her from leaving.

Inner pain cannot be seen on an X-ray. You cannot go to a pain management clinic to get an injection that will relieve your inner pain. Far too often, the inner pain is well hidden because most women in Zimbabwe have not felt that it is okay for them to openly express their inner pain.

Unfortunately, these women are the ones who have to live with this excruciating pain and the shame that accompanies it. I will call women like my mother and us, her children, victims.

We were victims, frightened for years by what we worried my father would do to our Mom, or what he would do to us, his children, if we ever rebelled or confronted him about his actions. We have had to deal with inner pain that is manifested and experienced in the form of serious depression, even to the extent of suicidal thoughts, or, during especially low times, wishing we were dead.

I know of women and children who were actually successful in their attempts to take their own lives. For them, it seemed that death was the most reasonable and easily attainable "treatment" or resolution to the emotional and mental pain they had to suffer through. I have watched my own mother reach a level of incredible hopelessness a number of times, and she has experienced an almost total loss of self-esteem over the last twenty years.

I have seen her struggling to tell her story, to speak of the emotional, physical, and spiritual pain she endured. It was very difficult for her to relay her story to others, much

Thriving Beyond the Tears - *Bruised and Never Broken* | Dr. Stem Mahlatini

less relate to those who believed that she had a good husband but that she was being stubborn in not accepting my father's other wives. So, in many cases, the women or children trapped in a polygamist situation will simply retreat into a world of their own, a world that often seems shrouded in darkness, a world with no hope of light.

They come to a very bleak place, one that is painful for the soul, the mind, and for one's emotions. Their inner pain runs deep, though it may be unseen by others. I realized that many women needed a forum in which they could feel free to discuss what they have gone through, how they have felt, and how they can reclaim their lives and their freedom and move Thriving Beyond the tears.

My prayer has been to find a way to help my mother heal and live out the rest of her days in peace. I am a therapist who has worked with many and helped many, but I felt helpless when it came to helping my own mother. I didn't know how to help myself, either. You might be asking, "Well, how were you affected by what your father did to your mother? Surely you shouldn't feel so much pain and resentment."

Yes, I do, and I will tell you why. There are certain feelings that all children who watch any of their parents splitting must endure. These feelings are greater when you watch your parents at odds with each other, like enemies. Mother always emphasized that no matter how she feels about Dad, we should always love him and treat him well, because he is our father. We have continued to do our part as their children.

The symptoms that I have struggled with are:

(a)   **Fear and Tension** – I have found myself feeling angry for years, but am only now realizing that this anger eventually caused emotional and even physical trauma for me and for my siblings. We all struggle with trusting our spouses. I have seen my sisters become angry with their husbands for no apparent reason. We have discussed how our tension and our fear of experiencing the things that happened to our mother have gotten in the way of our having loving, caring relationships with our respective husbands.

(b)   **Danger** – Although I was not home during the nine years in which the abuse included physical harm, my sisters have told me that they were always in danger of being beaten when Mother was being physically abused by Dad.

(c) **Confusion** – I have realized that, as children, we often received mixed messages. For example, I grew up hearing my dad criticizing others who were practicing polygamy. I could have sworn that my father would never, ever marry another wife. To my amazement, he did. I did not understand it. I was hurt. I was confused.

(d) **Hopelessness** – For years, my siblings and I were angry with my father. We despised his actions, and we despised him. Mother prayed and spoke to us, asking us to ease up on him because he is our father. Despite all that she had gone through, she still found it in her heart to want us to love our father regardless.

The good news is that we actually can go Thriving Beyond these tears, ladies. We can escape being victims. We do have the capacity, deep within each of us, to overcome the wrongs that were done to us and become strong, empowered women. We can regain our hope, our trust, and our faith.

The hardest part is reaching the point where we are ready to make the decision to pick up our baggage, hoist it out the door into the trash bin, and leave it there, ridding our lives of the inner pain that has haunted us. You see, that's just what the painful past is—trash!

The painful past keeps us from moving forward and stops us from walking the path of the true purpose for which we were created. I am ready to move on. I am ready for my God-given purpose. None of us was created for the sole purpose of being abused.

For those of us who have experienced physical, emotional, or spiritual abuse, let us take those terrible events and use them as a way to learn, heal, and help others, as God prepared us to do. This applies to all people who have experienced sexual abuse, as well.

There is a big difference between reliving your past and sharing your testimony for the benefit of others. This book was written for the sole purpose of sharing my testimony, sharing information of my family's life as a way to benefit all those who have had to live through similar experiences. The intent is a hopeful one: to lift others up.

The key is forgiveness. The way that my mother has come to experience her own angels who have helped her heal is both unconventional and amazing. When she came to the United States in 2009, I connected a home phone that was just for her to use. I had heard that there were prayer lines that had been started by Zimbabweans for Zimbabweans.

I gave her the numbers, and we both called from our respective phones to listen in on the prayers, testimonies, and Bible readings. I had no idea that the women on these prayer lines would be the Angels on my mother's path that would finally free her from her heavy heart.

She befriended a lot of women from the prayer line, and started to have daily phone prayers with as many as five people a day. It was during these intimate prayer calls that she decided she was going to volunteer her time preaching as well. I helped her with the Bible verses she needed and had her practice with me as her audience before she preached on the telephone. She was amazing.

I had thought she was still the shy lady with a poor sense of self-worth that I remembered. The prayer lines gave her confidence. One day, she felt comfortable sharing her story, and from that day onward she has had many blessing-filled moments praying with women who call her for prayer because they can relate to her story.

I have had people message me on Facebook saying they heard my mother preach on the telephone prayer line. (I will give the prayer line info at the end of this book.) To all those mothers who have prayed with my mother, who have listened to her story a million times, soothed her crying, and given her hope when you had no idea you were being her angel, I thank you from the bottom of my heart. Thriving Beyond all those tears is hope and encouragement for an anointed life that only God has in store for each of us.

In his own way, my father has been an angel to my mother and to us, his children. We are who we are today because of his love as a father and his care as a husband when the going was good. For that, Father, we thank you.

Now, on a lighter note, there are many people whom I have to acknowledge in this chapter. But first, let me remind you that each of us comes into this world with a special mission or purpose in life that only we can accomplish. It is the quest to find our mission, our purpose, that allows us to form meaningful relationships through which every person is an angel.

Every so often, some fortunate people may have a sense of what their purpose is, but many others have no idea. The few that might know may find out that they are not fortunate enough to have the encouragement or support they need. Instead, many of us are pushed into doing the things that our parents (or other people) feel is really best for us to be doing, and we end up ignoring our own vision of what we came here to do.

Coming to America allowed me to follow my own heart and gave me the will and the stamina to go against what others might have seen me doing with my life. In every path I have traveled, I now realize that there have been lots and lots of angels along the way—angels who, when I was lost, sad, and confused, always reminded me that I am here for a purpose.

It is amazing that when you start to think of life as having angels who have messages for you at all times, you begin to hear and see through a different lens. Life becomes meaningful.

For me, angels were the people I met and the inner voice I heard that would speak to me gently when I was working in jobs that I hated. I would be desperately wishing that there was something else I could be doing to pay the rent and put food on the table, and then I would hear the inner voice. It was at those moments, especially when this happened, that I honestly believed that there is more to life than what we settle for.

I started seeing that if I took time to listen to those angels around me, my life would take a turn for the better in due time. The key is having the courage to look, to listen, to be open and willing to take risks, and to begin working towards change.

The first angel I will mention who helped me to find my purpose and who taught me that there truly are angels along the way is a lady I will call Ms. Mary.

I was working at a local nursing home in Lowell, Massachusetts. After two years of working full-time and going to school for a degree in computer science, I met a family that was bringing their mother, Ms. Mary, into the nursing home.

Ms. Mary was in a wheelchair. She was crying and screaming at her children, asking them why they were not able to care for her at her home, and demanding to know why she had to be in a nursing home. She accused her children of not appreciating all she had done for them. It was a horrible thing to see and to hear. I asked them to take Ms. Mary to a private room, where I sat with them and talked to the family and tried to calm them all down.

I assured Ms. Mary that we would take good care of her and that we would treat her with respect and dignity, as if she were our own mother. I promised the children that we would do everything we could to make their mother comfortable and to help her feel at home. I spoke to them until the charge nurse ordered me to go back to my assigned work.

It was heart wrenching to leave them, but as I turned to go, I saw that Ms. Mary had stopped crying and she and her children were talking to one another without yelling. I made it a point to stop by the room again before I left that day, and I also went to see Ms. Mary every day to make sure she was all right.

I was just doing my job, but little did I know that I was on the path to finding my authentic self. One day, I stopped by to see Ms. Mary, and she asked me what courses I was taking in school. I told her that I was pursuing a computer science degree. She shook her head in disagreement, and said, "You are not a computer person! You are a social worker." She went on to explain that the way I had spoken to her and her family when they arrived at the nursing home that first day, reassuring them and then following up to be sure she was all right, was exactly what social workers do.

She told me that I had been at ease when talking to her and her family; it appeared to be natural for me to console and to help others. It was something I was really good at—I had helped her and her family through one of their darkest days. I was shocked! First of all, I had no idea that I could make a living by talking to people.

Secondly, I'd had no idea that I had made such an impact on Ms. Mary and her family. It was a wonderful feeling!

Ms. Mary suggested that I speak to the nursing home social worker and ask about a career in social work. I had long admired that social worker, the woman who always came in to help new families adjust to life at the nursing home.

But I have to confess that what I liked the most about her was the way she dressed. She wore pretty suits and high heels every day. I had no idea that what she did for a living was so exciting, or that I could actually be like her one day, and even wear suits like her!

The next day, I took Ms. Mary's advice and spoke to the social worker. The woman was extremely negative about her profession and about my chances for succeeding in it. She told me it was nearly impossible to get into any of the graduate programs without experience. She said it was especially difficult to get into the Boston University program that she had graduated from.

Well. I went straight to Ms. Mary's room and declared that I was going to be a social worker, and I even knew which college I was going to attend to earn my social work degree—Boston University. I was so excited to think that I could have a job I loved—a job I was born to do—that not even the social worker's lack of encouragement could stop me. To just be myself, talking to and helping people, and getting paid more money than I had ever made before—my excitement and optimism overshadowed every bit of that social worker's negativity.

I knew that if other people were able to get into Boston University's social work program, then it was possible for me, too. I am proud to say that I am today a graduate of Boston University. Thank you, my angel, Ms. Mary. I know that you are smiling in heaven to see the work I am now doing to help others live their best possible lives, just as you did for me.

I also found one of my late best friends in this nursing home, Edna Williams, who died of cancer a few years ago. It is because of her that I made it in the nursing home at all. I thought it was a very demeaning and difficult job until she showed me that if you do the job not as a job, but whole-heartedly, it becomes a joy, not a chore.
To my friends and mentors, thank you. You al

l have been my angels in your own ways. My apologies if I have left out any names; my heart is filled with gratitude. Thank you, my angels: Linda Eastman, Saru Furusa

Walsh, Rumbidzai Mkonto, Paulette Miller-Randolph, Rhonda Scott-Soudart, Eliza McCall Horn, Elisabeth Avila, Salvador Lainez, Frank Kashner, Mr. Wulf, Ms. June Marie Kershaw, Harold Marks, Carol McFarlane, Melanie Favors, Janean Furdock, Phillis A. Menschner, John Loblack, my uncle Sanda Sanganza, Steve Muzite, Antizah, the Sanganza and Mahlatini families, all the people I worked with at Fairhaven Nursing Home, Palm Manor Nursing Home, Tampa General Hospital, Salem High School in Massachusetts, Visions FM, Menschner & Associates Counseling Services, the Urban League of Central Florida, and the Department of Juvenile Justice.

Lessons Learned

This life is yours. Take the time to recognize the angels around you. Each person that you will meet has a lesson for you, be it good, or bad. Take advantage of all opportunities, because you never know where you might meet that life-changing angel along the way. Every situation in life has a purpose and a lesson to teach us.

There is a reason behind why things happen, why situations change, and why people do what they do. The lesson has been to embrace what life has to offer. My father's path was to be the way it is, so we have embraced it. My mother's path was to be the way it is, and we have also embraced it. Their two lives have woven a clearer path for me and for my siblings.

If I had not gone through what I have gone through, had not witnessed the pains and had not embraced the angels along the way, I would not have a memoir to share. I would not have a story to tell. I would not have a testimony to share with others who are experiencing the same pain. There is healing Thriving Beyond the tears.

A Dose of Motivation

My mother has shared with me some of the Bible verses and songs that have inspired and motivated her. I will share these with you so that you, too, can be motivated and pass them on.

Mother's Peace, found in Psalms 91

1 Whoever dwells in the shelter of the Most High will
   rest in the shadow of the Almighty.
2 I will say of the LORD, "He is my refuge and my
   fortress, my God, in whom I trust."

3 Surely he will save you from the fowler's snare and
   from the deadly pestilence.

4   He will cover you with his feathers, and under his wings you will find refuge;
    his faithfulness will be your shield and rampart.

5   You will not fear the terror of night, nor the arrow that flies by day,

6   Nor the pestilence that stalks in the darkness, nor the plague that destroys at midday.

7   A thousand may fall at your side, ten thousand at your right hand, but it will not come near you.

8   You will only observe with your eyes and see the punishment of the wicked.

9   If you say, "The LORD is my refuge," and you make the Most High your dwelling,

10 No harm will overtake you, no disaster will come near your tent.

11 For he will command his angels concerning you to guard you in all your ways;

12 they will lift you up in their hands, so that you will not strike your foot against a stone.

13 You will tread on the lion and the cobra; you will trample the great lion and the serpent.

14 "Because he loves me," says the LORD, "I will rescue him; I will protect him, for he acknowledges my name.

15 He will call on me, and I will answer him; I will be with him in trouble, I will deliver him and honor him.

16 With long life I will satisfy him and show him my salvation. "

7

Finding My True Purpose And Calling

"The biggest threat to our well-being is the absence of moral clarity and purpose."

Rich Sherman

Thriving Beyond the Tears - *Bruised and Never Broken* | Dr. Stem Mahlatini

Chapter 7
Finding My True Purpose
And Calling

Have you ever thought about who you are? What you stand for? Why you were born? I'm not talking about your family roles or work roles. You can be a friend, brother/sister, employee, boyfriend/girlfriend, husband/wife, partner, father/mother, son/daughter, all at the same time, but these are just a very small piece of who you are.

They don't represent who you are deep inside. Your inner self is who you really are on the inside. I had to have this chapter in the book because Thriving Beyond the tears is your true calling. Thriving Beyond the tears is your true joy, and only you can claim it.

To know your inner self is to know your purpose, your values, your visions, your motivations, your goals, and your beliefs. This is not what others have told you or what others have discovered in you, but what you have discovered in yourself. I notice that when I was in school, finding who I was and discovering my purpose were never part of the curricula I studied in all the years of schooling that I attended. Yet this is a major part of life. Knowing what I was created for and how to tap into my own self-knowledge would have helped me with the degree choices that I made.

Knowing your inner self requires a high level of self-examination and keen self-awareness. As Socrates famously said, "The unexamined life is not worth living." I realize the importance of being free of any past stress, hurts, resentments, anger, or frustrations when discovering who you really are. At the same time, the process of discovery never ends—it's a life-long journey.

Knowing Your Inner Self Comes From Self-Awareness

As I mentioned, knowing your inner self comes from truly knowing yourself, which is what we call self-awareness. Even if you do not have a clear picture of who you really are, it is important to take a look at your life and to see your responsibility for what has happened in your life. Every day is a journey in discovering who I am and what I stand for.

The more I uncover about myself, the more I am able to live and to do what I love. I have realized that before everything else, I am Sithembile Stem, as I am now affectionately known, or Thembie, as I was known by my grandparents. Sithembile means Hope, or to be hopeful, in my native language. I always say I am more than my identities.

I laugh because I have been told many a time that it is difficult for guys to date me because of my educational and professional accomplishments, when in truth all I am thinking is, "Well, I am more than all those accomplishments." It is a shame that people are discriminated against for having been diligent and persistent in preparing themselves educationally.

I admit it—there have been times when I was very confused about what my life's purpose was and about who I was. I have said in a previous chapter that my journey started in a nursing home, where Ms. Mary was the angel who told me that I was a social worker. Before she told me that, I had been struggling, trying to imagine what kind of life I would have working with computers, because I was pursuing a computer science degree at the time. I could not envision what my life would be like.

Deep down, I knew that computers were not my passion; I did not enjoy sitting at a machine for hours on end. I imagined, however, that somehow I would be paid more money that way, and the money would enable me to do what I wanted with my life.

It is surprising, thinking back, that the discovery of who you are and what you really enjoy doing has never been a priority—at least, not anywhere I have been. I have heard people complaining about their education, their work, their life, and their families, but have never heard a conversation that focuses on what it is that you are here on this earth for.

The two simple questions that helped me and which continue to help me are:
1.   What do you do for a living?
2.   What were you born to do?

What you do for a living is the safe option. That is the job that you do to pay the bills, to care for the family, and to provide for what we call all your day-to-day needs. It's comfortable, it's what you know, and it's what you've done for years.

Perhaps most significantly, it can't be all that horrible, because you're still doing it as you read this book. What you were born to do is, for many people, the frightening option. It requires us to shift away from what we know. It's uncertain whether you will get the money you need to survive or whether you will be successful. This is, however, what you enjoy doing the most. This is what would give you sleepless nights because it doesn't feel like work at all.

This is what inspired that anonymous quote, "Choose a job you love, and you will never have to work a day in your life." For most of us, the fear is "What if it doesn't work out?" You'll have left your day job—your security—for a dream that many will call silly. The scary part is, "Then what?" Do you go crawling back to reality, shamefully admitting that your dream, or your business idea, or your pride and joy, failed?

Many people hate the feeling of failure. They hate being talked about if it doesn't work, and they fear having wasted precious time going after this dream job or dream business.

This uncertainty, this fear of the unknown, scares many people to the point of never even trying to pursue their God-given talents. Many don't take action because they don't want to fail at whatever they love to do. I had to overcome this fear; I had to believe Ms. Mary and arrange to go through a social work program, where my true, authentic self would shine at Boston University in Massachusetts. I felt, though, that continuing with my degree in computer science and not changing to what I loved would be much worse.

Staying as a nurse's aide in the nursing home meant doing only what I had to do to pay the bills. My inner spirit knew I wanted to help people in a much larger capacity than as a worker in the nursing home. I could foresee myself becoming increasingly unhappy if I didn't pursue something I loved. Many people stay in unhappy positions, unhappy marriages, or unhappy relationships, and then blame other people for their unhappiness. We all have an obligation to ourselves first. We owe it to ourselves to take responsibility for what we want to do and what we have to do.

But wait. Is it that easy?

Unfortunately, it is not that easy for many. As human beings, we are influenced by other people a lot more than we usually acknowledge. When one is sad and in need of a friend's or a parent's advice, the influence is good, but there are many times when what has happened in the past puts restraints on our current relationships, which can make it difficult for some to find their true calling.

I recently read a book by Dr. Phillip C. McGraw called Self Matters: Creating Your Life from the Inside Out. In it, Dr. Phil discusses how the choices we make on a day-to-day basis help to promote happiness and to define our purpose. I couldn't agree more.

It's a very good, very detailed book as far as self-help books go, and I want to share a few statements that in particular really spoke to me.

On the subject of choices, he wrote:

"I have some bad news and I have some good news. The bad news is you are making the choices that have put you on this life circumstance; the good news is you are making the choices that have put you in this life circumstance."

Dr. Phil also includes a section on how our past shapes us and affects who we are and who we will become. He writes, "Social scientists tell us that the entire origin of your self-concept, and therefore determination of who you ultimately become in your life, can be traced to the events of a precious few days and the actions of an amazingly few key people involved in those happenings."

He goes on to say that out of the thousands of people you have met in your entire life, and despite all the good and bad things that have happened to you, the basis of who you are can be found rooted in only three things, which Dr. Phil describes as "ten defining moments, seven critical choices, and five pivotal people."

Leaving the nursing home and going to Boston University was only the beginning of my journey. I remember writing the entrance application essay with incredible passion and excitement. In the essay, I spoke of how much I love people. I love working with humans, in every capacity, and especially in times of distress. My goal is to create, as Oprah Winfrey put it, an "aha!" moment for myself and for those whom I serve and encounter.

I feel more satisfied when I encounter such a moment of enlightenment—a moment of increased courage, increased willpower, increased enthusiasm about life and a greater willingness to let that little light shine. I create this environment for my audience and for myself. My purpose is to be a messenger of Hope and Peace. God is my employer, and my passion is to serve him to the end.

I have realized that in everything I have done, putting him first has been the best decision of all. When I do what I do knowing that I am serving him, I rid myself of the stress caused by critics and negative people.

Whether you've already found whatever it is that you were born to do, or are just starting to take steps on the path towards embracing your true calling, my advice is to be grateful for life. I worked as a social worker in a hospital where I saw people who endured serious heart problems. Some of them lost their lives, dying prematurely at an age that should have been one of the physically strongest phases in their lives.

I also worked in hospice care, where I was privileged to speak with and minister to people in the last days of their lives. Being alive is a privilege, and when we learn to acknowledge the gift of life and aim to make the most of each day, we will no doubt find our true calling.

It is of no use to simply know that you are unhappy with what you are doing. You must also be willing to find an alternative. If you don't know one, or don't care enough to find out some other solution, you will remain stuck, doing the same old thing day in and day out.

I understand that sometimes we have to stick to what we are able to do because we don't have the right papers; that is how it was for me at one point. What I don't understand are those who pray about getting papers, or who complain about their inability to obtain the right work papers, and who then fail to work at finding some other solution.

Everything in life has the potential to erect a roadblock that either requires you to think outside of the box or that forces you to act in a way that is different from the norm. When the situation hurts us long and deep enough, we do whatever is necessary to get what we need. Ask yourself: What is it that you need in order to be able to pursue your true calling? What can you do about it? Who can you talk to about it? Who can you pray with about it? Now, act on this information. Do whatever it is that you have to do.

There is always a little voice within each of us, a voice that keeps nagging us, keeps ringing in our ears, and keeps us unhappy by making us uncomfortable in any situation. The situation could involve almost anything: cooking, painting, starting a business, writing, going back to school, working to improve a relationship, etc. Suddenly, we realize the source of our sadness, anger, and dissatisfaction with our lives. It comes from not finding fulfillment in either the choices we have made or in what we do for a living.

At Boston University I realized that working with people was my calling. I worked as an intern at Women Inc., where I worked with women who were recovering from addiction.

I was changed by my experience with counseling them, just as they changed as a result of my counseling. That is my calling. I enjoy coaching people and counseling people because as they heal, I am healed as well. My work included working with adolescents. Now, looking back, I am amazed at how my life path has so often involved working with women and youth.

In finding your passion, as I found mine, I want to make it clear that some people are clearly content and happy with working at their job and doing what they are doing. That is admirable, and as long as you are happy and content with where you, understand that the key to contentment is not the pay, but rather is your ability to do what you do with passion and happiness.

It is knowing Thriving Beyond a shadow of doubt that the work you do is the best you can do and that you are happy with where you are. When you have found your passion, you sleep at night knowing what it is you were born to do, and you do not have moments of wishing you were doing something else.

Even though I worked for many different human service agencies, programs, and hospitals over the years, I loved what I did. The pay was great. My only issue with my job was that I wanted to impact more people. I wanted to travel. I wanted the freedom to teach, to speak, and to connect with many more people.

I also wanted to work for myself and to have the freedom to do more with my time. I left job after job for new opportunities. I went to school to get further educated, but I still was not satisfied with working for anyone else. I love Florida, and when I finished my doctorate degree, I knew it was time to shift and to move into my true calling. I had to sacrifice the love I felt for Florida and move back to Massachusetts so that I could work for myself and do what I love most—coaching, speaking, training, and traveling. It was what I was meant to do.

I had to move, in part, because I did not want to be one of those people who will look back at the end of their life and realize that they should have pursued their true calling. Instead, I listened to that inner voice and paid attention to the outer stress that said I wanted to work for myself. Unlike many who, I suspect, will regret not having taken chances, I wanted to try.

I would leap at the chance to work for myself and to help more people, and allow God to do the rest. I, however, was afraid. I was afraid that I might be taking a big step backward, because I had left Boston sixteen years before to seek a better life in Florida. My friends in Florida told me I wouldn't last long in the cold; they said I'd soon give up and come back.

But I didn't listen to them. I believed I would last in the cold, if I was doing the work that was meant for me. I have since learned that you cannot mess with a made-up mind. I was determined; I had made up my mind that I was going to move back to Massachusetts, and I was certain that I would find a way to make it. It wasn't easy. I was embarrassed to be moving back, and I was nervous at the thought of how I would even get started, but the thought of "What if I succeed?" was stronger than my concerns, so I moved.

What is this monster, called 'fear,' that we all talk about it when we discuss whether we should try pursuing our dreams, going after our heart's desires, or taking the risks that we need to take? What is it about fear that keeps many people captive, trapped by tears and pain, seemingly unable to move Thriving Beyond the tears into a brighter future?

It is truly scary how fear gets in the way of many of us moving ahead with our lives. We fear giving up our security, or we fear the failure that might result from pursuing our dreams. In some cases, we fear our own success, or fear having to maintain that success over years or decades.

We fear what people will say or what they will think. We worry that we might not have what it takes to do what we are driven to do, even when we have all the necessary qualifications and more. I talk about fear again because fear is such a barrier to so many people. No matter how many books you have read, how much education you've received, or how much you are ministered to, if you don't conquer your fears, you will not move ahead. If you never move ahead, you will not be able to find your true calling before your time on this earth is up.

Think of a fly. It's such a little creature, but it is amazingly fearless and powerful. Fear is like the little fly; it can bite a big man or woman and leave them scratching and moaning from pain. We must recognize that we have the option of swatting the fly and stepping away. We cannot allow these fears and concerns to stop us from living our dream life.

Any fearful excuse we can give for not doing something can be thought of as a small fly and swatted off.

I noticed that for many years, whenever I was about make a change in my life—even if it was simply from one job to another, similar job—I felt scared. Because of my fear, it took a long time for me to truly make up my mind. I had a secure job in Florida.

I was content, in some ways, with where I was. But I wasn't truly content. To find my true calling, I had to move when I needed to move. I had to say "Yes, Lord," and trust in him. So at last, when I most needed to make a change and return to Massachusetts, my dream was bigger than my fears.

As foreigners, we have a different mission than most, I think. We are survivors, so when we get a job that requires us to show up, put in some work, and get paid, we show up. We show up for the paycheck that allows us the freedom of money we did not have back home.

The paycheck, the benefits, and the health insurance usually keep many people from moving. It is the security that comes from having this stability in our lives that usually keeps us from finding our true calling. I gave it all up, and moved with just a couple suitcases and my car.

Two weeks after I arrived in Massachusetts, my car died. I had no job and no money to fix it. I found a part-time job that paid very little and worked to get enough money to buy another used car and to seek another, better-paying job. When you decide to pursue your passion, your calling, you will face many stumbling blocks along the way. There will be disappointments and setbacks. It will not be easy. But it is worth it.

The answer is already within you. Your job is to face the fear that is trying to stop you and follow your passion anyway. If you haven't yet found the work you were meant to do, keep searching, keep praying, and be ready to act when you finally find what you want.

It is so good to be doing what you love. I know this because after I moved to Massachusetts, I worked menial jobs here and there until I found a job that paid really well at a local hospice agency. The pay was more than I had ever been paid before, but my calling was far greater than the pay I was earning. So I saved that money and eventually used it to pay for an office with one of my angels, Helen Hawk, a licensed psychotherapist in private practice.

I paid a very minimal fee, as I had applied for provider privileges with many health insurance companies in

Massachusetts. This process took hours and hours of writing. I remember my nieces, Charles and Chantelle, asking me why I never slept. I remember my sister Nikki and her boyfriend Teddy asking me why I had so much paperwork every day.

I worked part time on my dream and full time on the job that paid the bills. My part-time work was my future, because once I succeeded in it, I would be free to pursue my calling and my passion. The profits that owning a business would bring excited me, as well; I was tired of living from paycheck to paycheck.

I explained to my nieces that I was working so hard so that one day, whenever I open my mailbox, every envelope inside would be a check from my patients' health insurance paying me for having counseled them. I told my nieces that I had spoken to Helen, who said she had been doing counseling in a private practice for a long time, and the freedom to work when she wanted was unsurpassed.

I started imagining the checks in the mail instead of just bills. I started envisioning myself traveling, conducting seminars, and taking on speaking engagements. I was already seeing myself writing books and inspiring people through the books and through television and radio broadcasts. My mind was made up.

I remember going through snowstorms in tears. I did not have a boyfriend to help me shovel my car out of the snow, and most of the time my brothers-in-law were at work when I called them looking for help.

So I rolled up my sleeves and dug myself out. As I shoveled snow in the wake of one of these storms, I realized that over the past months, I had been digging myself free of my old ways of thinking and living. I was freeing myself from old expectations, becoming more than I had thought I could ever be. At that moment, I knew: I was going to make it no matter what.

I was doing fulfilling work, but needed to expand my territory. As one of my great mentors, Les Brown, says, "If you take responsibility for yourself, you will develop a hunger to accomplish your dreams." When you are hungry, no one can stop you.

The questions you should ask yourself as you read this chapter are these: Are you truly happy with where you are in life? Are you happy to work in a career that is fulfilling and enjoyable?

Because when you really love your work, you greet the day with a smile that can brighten a whole room. They say you won't need a clock to wake you. You will wake when you need to wake, all on your own, because you love what you do.

I have conducted training seminars and done speaking engagements where people have asked me if it is too late to make a change. Maybe you are one of those people, and are asking yourself whether it is too late for you. Maybe you believe that you've somehow missed your calling and now you are thinking that you should pursue it now—after all, you are not getting any younger.

I believe the 19th century writer George Eliot got it right when she said, "You're never too old to be what you might have been." My first coach, Sasha ZeBryk, laughed when I told her that at the age of forty-five, I was too old to try something new. That was two years ago. She empowered me to pursue my speaking passion because she herself had started in her fifties, and she is doing very well and going steadily forward.

When I left Zimbabwe, I believed—as many of my fellow Zimbabweans also believed— that my purpose was to be a good person, to set a good example, to get an education and get married. I was supposed to stay out of trouble and then, at some arbitrary point in life, I was supposed to contribute to society. I didn't think that my purpose was to set goals and pursue them; I felt like my purpose was to take whatever life threw at me, wait for something good to happen to me, and then, after a lifetime of waiting, die.

Obviously, I no longer believe those things. Instead, I now believe that we all can think and act on our own merits. We do not at any point in our lives have to settle for anything. We can choose to tolerate something until we can do better, or we can find better ways or alternate solutions. But even when we choose to wait, it is a choice. We are not waiting passively. We are waiting, and watching for a chance to make our situation better.

My belief is that none of us have special birthmarks that allow for special privileges in fulfilling our life's calling. I believe that if we build enough faith and strength within us to go after what we need, then we are bound to get that and more. There will be hard work required of you along the way while you become the person you were meant to be. In the lessons I learned, I will share with you the steps I found to be helpful in uncovering my inner self.

There are those who will say, "Well, my situation makes it harder to find my purpose or to be what I was meant to be." To many, it is difficult even to fathom having the passion to find out what they are meant to do on this earth. To them, I leave this quote from Richard Bach: "Here is the test to find whether your mission on earth is finished. If you're alive, it isn't."

Lessons Learned

Here are some steps which I found to be useful in uncovering my inner self:

- Being open to continuously learning and growing as a person.

- Putting myself in fearful situations in order to get to where I want to go.

- Constant reflection on the lessons learned and looking within for inner strength.

- Looking Thriving Beyond what I am told in order to discover what I want for myself

- Listening to my gut feeling when it arises.

- Assuring myself that I am as good as those who have made it or better.

- Not blaming myself when I didn't make it; I knew I was doing my best.

- Believing that all things are possible to those who believe.

- Being patient with myself when I didn't make it.

- Celebrating each step I took towards my dream, no matter how big or small the step.

- The longer you put off following your heart, the harder it is to leave the supposed "security" of the place you are at.

- I learned that you have to move from where you are to get to where you want to be. As John A. Shedd said, "A ship in a harbor is safe, but that is not what ships are for."

- "Happiness is an individual matter. When you are able to bring relief, or bring back the smile to one person, not only that person profits, but you also profit. The deepest happiness you can have comes from that capacity to help relieve the suffering of others. ... Nothing compels us, except the joy of sharing peace, the joy of sharing freedom from our pain, freedom from worries, freedom from craving, which are the true foundations for happiness." Thich Nhat Hanh, Vietnamese Buddhist teacher & author

- "Risk! Risk! Anything! Care no more for the opinion of others, for those voices. Do the hardest thing on earth for you. Act for yourself. Face the truth." Katherine Mansfield

They say with age comes wisdom. I am a work in progress. I still make mistakes and I still have doubts, but my continued passion for my dream is bigger than the fears. My refusal to be negative and my willingness to work on improving my actions and reactions have resulted in my becoming more and more in harmony as a person. Today, I'm at a place where my outward identities are well in line with who I am on the inside.

While there's definitely still room for further alignment, my inner and outer selves are quite congruent with one another. And all this didn't happen by chance. It came about as a result of conscious effort. I now monitor what I say to myself and other people. I pat attention to how I handle different situations. I constantly have to tell myself that I don't have to be defensive when people ask me on why I always emphasize the importance of being positive as a catalyst to leading the life of your dreams.

People have sometimes accused me of being too positive, but many are now seeing that I have been in Boston for four years without wishing for even a single day that I was back in Florida. I am a survivor, not a quitter, and by believing that "Yes, I can do this," I have made life's transitions more bearable.

A Dose of Motivation

As Oprah Winfrey once said, "You are not the product of your circumstances. You are a composite of all the things you believe, and all the places you believe you can go. Your past does not define you.

You can step out of your history and create a new day for yourself. ... Even if every single possible bad thing that can happen to you does, you can keep going forward." I agree one hundred percent. When you decide to create a life that is of your own choosing, you are certain to make some changes, despite the tears and pain.

- What makes you feel most alive?
- What's something you do that makes you feel like everything is right in the world?
- What gives you a feeling of satisfaction?

When it comes to finding your true calling, set peace of mind as your highest goal and aim to do things that give you a feeling of total bliss.

8

When The Student Is Ready The Teacher Arrives

"Create a definite plan for carrying out your desire and begin at once, whether you are ready or not, to put this plan into action."

Napoleon Hill

Chapter 8
When The Student Is Ready
The Teacher Arrives

I believe we all have a higher power that we believe in or a universe that is always looking out for us. I believe in God and believe that the best way for me to write this chapter is for me to be open about my belief in God and his powers over my life. This is also a way for me to explain my role in the waiting. You are the student, and your teachers are the people, the blessings, the opportunities, and the rewards that will show up in your life when you have prepared yourself and readied yourself to receive them.

I have found that there have been times in my life where opportunities have come along and I just wasn't ready to take advantage of what was right in front of me. If you have ever had that experience, you know that it's frustrating and demoralizing. If you are really serious about going from your dreams to reality, then you will need to ready yourself to receive these opportunities.

What am I saying when I talk about being ready? Let's say you are working as a nurse's aide or a personal care attendant, but you really want to be a writer. What do you need to do in your free time? That is correct. WRITE! You need to be practicing for your dream, whether by writing research writers, reading books, studying grammar, taking writing classes, etc.

The point is that in every free moment, every chance you find, you need to be submerging yourself in writing. Why? Because you need to be doing all you can to be prepared and ready for your dream.

You never know when an opportunity will present itself. It could be tomorrow, or next year, or next week. In the case of our example with the nurse's aide, what if someone had offered her a book deal? If she had been using every free moment to hone her craft, she would be ready for that golden moment. If she had been only wishing and hoping, but not doing anything to get ready, that once-in-a-lifetime chance would have slipped away. Since you never know what tomorrow may hold, it only makes sense to work toward your goals however and whenever you can.

I am sure that I am not the only one who continuously prays for the Lord's blessings in all areas of my life and who waits on him for his answers. We all want to be blessed by the Lord. We all want to be successful, free, and happy. We all want to joyful, peaceful, and healthy. While I believe that God wants to bless us all, I also believe that God wants to teach you and me how to fight and how to be survivors. For you to be successful at anything, you have to fight for it, to work hard at it.

You have to claim it with all your might. If we do not have a deep foundation of faith, we may have difficulty withstanding the harsh storms and icy winds of adversity which unavoidably come to each of us. Experiencing death puts us through a period of tests, a time to prove ourselves worthy to return to the presence of our Heavenly Father for his guidance and protection.

In order for us to be tested, we must face challenges and difficulties. These can break us, and the surface of our souls may crack and crumble in difficult times, shaking our faith to the core. God wants us to be tough and diligent. I have learned that God is my rock, my strength and my power.

He makes my way perfect; this I believe. I have seen his hand at work in many areas of my life, from the time I was born to now living in a foreign land. He has made my feet like the feet of deer, and set me on high places which only him could do. I have learned through it all that we are created to conquer. It is not God's intention for us to be lazy, to be afraid, to be average, or to struggle.

There is no way you can receive the blessings God has planned for your life without you fighting the obstacles, the challenging moments and the challenging events that block the way to your promised land, your calling, your ideal life. There is no way your blessings can come when you are not prepared to receive them. Preparation is key.

You see, that is why people who are procrastinators never accomplish anything in life. Because they are looking for ways to reach their goals without struggling or overcoming the challenges in their way. I believe that there are various tests that we all have to pass before the will Lord release your blessings into your life. As I write this memoir, I am having great revelations about my own life.

I have waited to be married and to have children forever, as far as I know, but to the Lord time is not of the essence until he is ready to release that blessing. I have yearned to be a world-renowned motivational and inspirational speaker, trainer, television and radio persona, and that, too, had to wait until I went through the lessons of life.

I was not blessed with the ability to live my dream until I could understand the meaning of God's blessings. Let me share with you why it is important to be ready and what God's blessing means:

1. His blessing means responsibility. Responsibility means total surrender to his will and his ways. The questions are: Are you a responsible person? God wants to bless us, but we have to understand that the more he blesses us, the more we will have and the more we will own, hence we will be more responsible for ensuring good use of his blessings.

   Have you noticed that People who have no car have no need for gas. To be honest, being blessed means hard work, but if we focus on his will, I think the path will be clear and the yoke will not be heavy. Everything God gives us requires maintenance. God gave Adam the garden, but he still had to work it.

2. His blessing means stewardship and sharing with others. Many people think that God blesses them to keep his blessings for themselves, but I have learned that no matter how much God blesses you, you must know that you are not the owner; you are just the overseer of his blessings.

Luke 12:48 states,

"For unto whomsoever much is given, of him shall be much required; and to whom men have committed much, of him they will ask the more."

3.   His blessing means humility. I always think of my favorite hymn from when I was a Sunday school teacher. It is called "Humble Yourself before the Lord."

The lyrics go like this:

Humble yourself before the Lord,
he will lift you up.
He will lift you up, he will lift you up, if you only
Humble yourself before the Lord,
he will lift you up.

Let me tell you there is a difference between humbling yourself and receiving your blessings, and having excess money. A man of God said,

"A rich man without Christ is a poor man with excess money."

If you are one of those people who are always weeping over rejection and misunderstanding, if you are always upset over who doesn't accept you into their circle anymore, then you better get used to it.

As the Lord blesses you, people will criticize you, and you will face even more rejection. I have learned it is best to be like David, who said in Psalm 27:5,

"For in the time of trouble He shall hide me in his pavilion: in the secret of His tabernacle shall he hide me; He shall set me up on a rock."

This is the place where we find comfort and peace in God from the bombardment of cynical people's criticism and the constant pressure to perform. This takes humility.

My mother and the women of God from the telephone prayer line have been my shield. I have been prayed for, so I know I am protected by his blood as I embark on my motivating and inspiring journey through speaking, training, coaching, radio, and television.

4.   His blessing means serving—being of service. A person who is blessed has to be ready to be of service and must not have any problem with being a servant of the Lord. Jesus says whosoever wants to be the greatest in the kingdom of God must be the servant of you all. Matthew 20:26 says,

"Yet it shall not be so among you; but whoever desires to become great among you, let him be your servant."

Many think that when you have been elevated and blessed you are better than others, when instead it simply means you are one with many.

5.   His blessing means being an example for others. When you are blessed, God wants you to be a good role model for other people. As Christians, we are blessed especially when we are called to be role models for those around us. Paul says in Philippians 3:17,

"Brethren, join in following my example, and note those who so walk, as you have us as a pattern." *When you are blessed, many people are watching you.*

They want to be like you. When you are truly blessed of the Lord, you will be impacting other people's lives by your presence and by your example. That is why the Lord wants all of us to be blessed. Many are called, and few are chosen, but the blessing is there for all who are willing to be vessels of his calling.

6. His blessing means compassion and empathy. A truly blessed person has compassion for other people. He or she knows that the blessing is because of God's compassion. The blessing means one has to be compassionate about others and empathetic towards them.

7. His blessing means faithfulness. The reason God keeps blessing some people is because they are faithful to him in little things. You need to be faithful to receive more blessings from the Lord. Luke 19:17 says,

"And he said to him, 'Well done, good servant; because you were faithful in a very little, have authority over ten cities.'" When you are faithful in little things, then God will entrust you with more.

8.   His blessing means honesty. A truly blessed person knows the importance of giving. If you get rich through deceit, the Bible says death can result from it.

9.   His blessing means giving. A truly blessed person knows the importance of giving. Contrary to what others think of financial abundance, my prayer is that I am richly blessed so that I can give and provide services to many. My dream is to build vocational programs, homes, shelters, hospitals and schools for street kids in Zimbabwe.

These children touch my heart because their parents died, mostly because of untreated illnesses such as AIDS, cancer, heart problems, and kidney or lung problems. Proverbs 19:17 says: "He who has pity on the poor lends to the LORD. And he will pay back what he has given."

10.   His blessing means patience. I know those who know me will laugh at this part and say, "Yes, Stem needs to learn patience." I am open to the idea of learning to be patient. Some people, like me, struggle with patience deficiency syndrome. Because I am ready for my blessing, I have had to

learn patience, because unless I am patient—or so many people have told me—I will have difficulty handling wealth. You see, when God blesses you, then you will have to deal with the problems that go with wealth.

One of these is that very wealthy individuals have always had people around them, some waiting for them, and others waiting on them. You need patience to be able to manage both the wealth and those around you. The truth is, if you are not patient, then you will destroy yourself and others. Galatians 6:9 says,

"So don't get tired of doing what is good. Don't get discouraged and give up, for we will reap a harvest of blessing at the appropriate time." *(Living Translation)*

His blessing means thankfulness and appreciativeness. Some people have difficulty appreciating little things. I have been blessed to have had four years Thriving Beyond my graduate studies to start being a blessing to my parents by helping them financially as much as I can. It is still on a very small scale, but I am grateful for the ability to show them my appreciation and thankfulness.

The greatest gift has been seeing them get to the point of being thanked and blessed for how they raised my siblings and me. We are children who work hard and know that we have to be thankful of the little things we have so that God can bless us with more.

When I first encountered this quote, "When the student is ready, the teacher arrives," I did not find any meaning in it. I thought the teacher has to be the one looking out for the student, that the teacher has to actively involved in teaching others, and in the process, the student will learn. If the teacher never takes action, the student never learns—or so I thought. I realize now that getting ready for what you want is more important before the teachers arrive.

It was only recently that I gained an understanding of this. Most of us, if not all of us, hear what we are ready to hear. If we are not ready to receive, then nothing, no matter how sound the advice may be, will get into our head. It is ourselves who choose to filter out information.

I have learned that the teacher is always ready to teach, but the student is not always ready to listen. Some people are blessed enough to open up to life and receive their teachings later in life, but they often express regret, saying to themselves, "Why didn't I know this earlier?" It is because the student was not ready. I missed a lot of opportunities for growth earlier in my life because I was not ready; the student was not ready.

My advice to you is to be a ready student—the answer that you seek will come to you. Negative talk, negative thinking, low self-worth, and an inability to forgive are some of reasons we get stuck for so long in a situation where we are unhappy, but not ready to receive.

Being a ready student means opening up to the fact that we must become flexible. When others speak to us, we must be willing to consider their words. When we receive a blessing we did not expect, we should consider that it may be the best blessing for us at that moment, whether we were aware of this or not.

This statement is another true revelation of what is happening in my life as I write this. I continue to be grateful and receptive. I thank God for answering my prayers, because I believe there are no coincidences in life; every step we take is made for a purpose.

Our role is to be open and ready, and when we are, then the teacher will arrive. This means that when you start arguing with someone or ridiculing what they have to say, you should stop yourself because there might be a message for you being delivered at that moment.

I love music so you will see that throughout this memoir I have shared a lot of lyrics that helped me along the way. I like the song "God's Got A Blessing (With Your Name On It)" by Norman Hutchins because knowing that God has a special blessing for me has helped me open myself to his will. It has helped me to look at each person I meet as a teacher.

Lessons Learned

- I have learned that I do not walk alone. You do not walk alone, either. As you walk through life, always walk toward the light, and the shadows of life will fall behind you.

- I have learned that the Lord says, "Come unto me, come learn of me, and come follow me."

- I learned that by taking serious action toward achieving your dream, you are sending a message to God that you have unwavering faith that your dreams will come true and that you are willing to do the work to make that happen and to allow him to make it happen for you.

- I have learned that my taking action is setting the wheels of the Universe in motion, making me a magnet for the experience I desire.

- I learned that submerging myself in my dream, my vision, and taking action—that is, writing, speaking, booking myself and constantly visualizing myself doing what I love full time—brings my teachers faster. I see opportunities far more quickly, which helps my mission.

- I learned that no matter what they are, my dominant thoughts and feelings will find a way to manifest in my life. I become what I think about most of the time. This is an example of what they call the law of attraction. You attract what you think about most of the time.

I learned that, essentially, you will live the life that you predict you will live. What do you want most? Think about it and take actions to get you closer to your goal. Having goals is your way of moving towards your dream life.

What is a Dream life for you? Knowing your passion, your dream; will help expedite fruition of your dream life.

A Dose of Motivation

Questions are one great way to get yourself ready. Take a moment and write your answers to the questions below.

1.   If your dream opportunity or big break came knocking on your door. Would you be ready to seize it?

2.   If not, why not?

3.   What can you do today that will get you one step closer to being ready?

4.   What things would you have to add to your daily routine this month to get yourself prepared?

5.   What activities, ideas or even relationships would you need to rid yourself to get you on the right track?

6.   What are you going to do today to keep yourself ready and open to learn so that you never have to miss your teachers?

9

Living Life Despite It All

"Change will not come if we wait for some other person or some other time. We are the ones we've been waiting for. We are the change that we seek."

Barack Obama

Thriving Beyond the Tears - *Bruised and Never Broken* | Dr. Stem Mahlatini

Chapter 9
Living Life Despite It All

The journey called life has not been easy for me over the past twenty-five years, and it has been even harder for my mother. The emotional struggles we've faced have taken their toll at times, and together, we have gone through the depression, the anger, the confusion and the unwillingness to forgive.

I have been blessed to live with my mother over the last two years. I was away for twenty-two years before I brought her to live with me so that she could get the healthcare she needs and so she could take a break from the monotony of being in Zimbabwe without her husband or her biological children. All seven children are in the USA, so it was very difficult for her to hear people telling her that she was going to die alone, since none of her children were coming back to Zimbabwe.

However, she has had the company of my cousins, her sister's children. Her being with us today is a sign of the love she has received from them, especially Sisi Joyce Nyagura-Dozva and Ronika Grace Nyagura. Lord knows how much you mean to me, to mother, and to everyone in our family; I thank you both and I want more than anything for God to bless you abundantly with your heart's wishes. For all my nephews and nieces who are in Zimbabwe—too many of you to mention—I also want you to know that without your help, we would not have Mom (Gogo as she is affectionately known) here with us.

Being in the USA makes it so difficult to care for relatives, especially elderly parents, while here. I do not recall ever hearing of anyone putting their parents in a nursing home; we always took care of our own. I never thought I would get to a point where I could see my mother at peace, living well despite her pain and past struggles. Challenging times in our lives are meant to become the experiences that help us grow into strong, God-dependent children.

I never knew that the initial adjustment would be as difficult as it was during the first months I lived with her. I was excited, but I was also unsure of what to expect. I had to get to know her all over again, and she had to get to know me, too, because it had been over twenty years since we had lived together. When we experience difficult moments and things aren't going our way, it's tempting to find blame and to be sad and depressed. Thoughts of survival and of living life despite what is happening are put on hold. For years, we all had put our ambitions—our happiness and joy—on hold. But now it's time to move on. We are survivors and we are here. Life is about living; now, we are ready to live. In the end, the choice is for each individual to choose how they would like to live their life.

I blamed my father for the choices he made that hurt my family and my mother. I blamed his other wives, too, and I blamed those who supported his practice. All this time, the blame I felt was holding me back from receiving my ultimate blessings. I now realize that the choice to move on is mine to make. The choice to let go is all mine. Interestingly, living with Mother, watching her dropping the emotional baggage she has carried for years and choosing to live a better life, has helped me to move forward and work toward dropping my own emotional baggage.

She moved Thriving Beyond her tears of sadness by overcoming her shyness and taking turns preaching on the Zimbabwe prayer lines. She has told her story, and many other women have testified about going through the same pain she has gone through. Having the courage even to tell the story is itself a sign of healing. Having the power to dismiss other people's negative opinions and scrutiny has been perhaps her greatest achievement toward finding her true self. My mother used to be bothered by the smallest of things: people who would talk about her situation, who said she was a fool to allow this second wife to stay in Mom's home and conceive her first child there.

Today, she laughs about the way people treated her, seeing her as a weak woman with no backbone. We both agree that they were correct; she had no backbone—then. Today, Mother would speak up before anyone could say anything. Today, she can stand tall and preach the word of the Lord with conviction. Her sharing is where the most healing has occurred. We both have learned the hard way that happiness and joy are dependent on our willingness to let ourselves live and to be happy.

We all hold the power to choose life in spite of all that is happening around us. We are here to be the source of happiness in our own life. We cannot look to other people to be the source of happiness in our lives, or to make it possible for us to live meaningful lives. We must rely on ourselves.

Yes, we were emotionally victimized. Yes, we were disappointed with how the family split. Such is life. We now realize that the storm we kept raging for years is over.

Now, it's time to live, and to live deliberately, to live on purpose. It is time to push forward in faith, believing and expecting good things. Our energy is being used to help us thrive. Deep down, we now know that even though sometimes fierce emotions are stirred up, we know God is in the midst it all. God is opening supernatural doors for us as we let go of our anger and resentment. We survived, but we cannot remain victims for life.

Mother says the only thing she has left to do on this earth is praise the Lord and enjoy the rest of her days. I couldn't agree more. It doesn't matter what happened. We still love our father, and God has a way to bless us, despite it all.

For many people, it is easy to start thinking of themselves as stuck in place because other people have hurt them or taken advantage of them. But in many cases, this mentality is not helpful. It leads to thinking that an opportunity isn't worth taking when it is.

This chapter will hopefully minister to your hearts and help to allow God to work miracles in your lives. The journey has been long in coming for my family. It is time to shift from fear to faith, from pain to pleasure, from our victim/survivor mentality to a happier mental place where we can be assertive, God-fearing women and men of God.

Being with Mother has had me wondering why people stay in the victim mode or mentality for a long time. Below are the reasons I have encountered.

Attention and validation. Throughout the years, I have noticed that the more we acknowledged and talked about how much we hurt, the more people felt sorry for us and Mother. It was great to know that people were there for us and understood our pain. The fact is, yes, you can always get good feelings from other people, as they are concerned about you and may try to help you out.

On the other hand, it may not last, as people quickly get tired of it. My father's remarrying is now a blessing for all of us. All of us seven siblings and Mother have had to work hard and aim to achieve the best in order to keep our sanity. I now realize that staying in the victim mentality meant:

(1)   That we didn't have to take risks. We didn't have to work hard at bettering ourselves. We didn't have to start businesses or families. When you feel like a victim, you tend to not take action and then you don't have to risk, for example, rejection or failure. Mother was so dependent on Dad that when he left, the pain she endured became the fire she needed to

take charge of life. In some ways, it brought out the best in her.

(2) We didn't have to take the sometimes-heavy responsibility for our lives. Taking responsibility for you own life can be hard work; you have to make difficult decisions and stick to them. In the short term, it can feel easier to not take personal responsibility and to convince yourself that action is not possible because you are a victim.

But this is self-deceit, because now you cannot grow personally or professionally, and if you cannot grow, you can't do what you need to do to live the life you were meant to live.

(3) We felt we were right. Our father was wrong; we were right. When you feel like the victim and like everyone else—or just someone else—is in the wrong and you are in the right, then that can lead to pleasurable feelings.

For years, we didn't talk to our father. He had wronged the family, so we rebelled against him. This only made us more distant and deepened the strong feelings of victimhood that we felt.

We have learned to be okay with not being the victims anymore, just as we saw Mother becoming okay with not being a victim. She has had to break out of that mentality. She experienced a sort of emptiness within, an emptiness one sometimes feels when they first let go of victim thinking.

The emptiness has not been there for long, though, because she is filling it with hope and prayer with the help of the women from the telephone prayer line. Mother used to spend hours and hours each day thinking about how wrong things been and how badly her live has gone. My siblings and I spent sporadic, irregular hours griping on the phone about our father's actions.

The more we held on to these negative thoughts and brought them out in conversation, the more resentful we became. The pain only felt worse. We bred more negativity in everything we did. The key, I learned, is to look for the blessings around me and reach for the strength within me.

I have learned to live with a purpose; despite everything. This choice is open to all of us, regardless of what our circumstances are.

Time to Take responsibility for Our Life.

For years, even us children looked at Mother and wondered why she had such low self-esteem. We wondered why she allowed Father to walk all over her—let alone his second wife, who, for the life of me, agreed to go destroy my mother's life, and then had to do it in Mother's face.

She even did it in Mother's own home, the home that she had built up with her sweat and hard work. We have forgiven her, too; the reasons she had for her actions are between her and her God. We are ready to take responsibility for our lives, and are determined that no weapon aimed against us shall prosper.

Why do people often have self-esteem problems? I'd say that one of the biggest reasons is their upbringing. Their values and beliefs play a big role in the choices they make later. Unfortunately, their laid back, non-confrontational attitude impacts their decision to not take responsibility for their lives.

Mother herself had no idea she could have the life she has now, stress-free and independent of emotional and physical abuse. She has had to roll up her sleeves and take charge of the family. You have done a great job, Mother.

"Kushinga Hakunyadzise mhai, tinotenda nekushinga kwenyu, nesacrife yeupenyu hwenyu kuti isu vana venyu tiwane runyararo." Mother, thank you for your love and prayers; your sacrifice will not go unnoticed. We love you, Mommy, and hope that we have and will continue to make you proud.

We wish and hope to have a Mahlatini Family Reunion Bash in Zimbabwe and invite Dad back to celebrate life with all of us. We have life, and that is more important than complaining, whining, and carrying on about the past. We are bigger than our past. We are bigger than our circumstances.

Looking back, I don't know any other way we could have come to this point of healing. Life is a journey. We had to go through what we went through to finally come to this point of overcoming the pains brought to us by victimization. I now know that the hurt will not stop on its own; it will not end until you wise up and choose to take responsibility for your life. There is really no way around it.

We had to feel the pain. The key now is to take responsibility for creating and making manifest our own joy and happiness.

It is interesting that for years we have sat down with my siblings and vented about how we have not seen the proceeds of our hard work or benefited from the personal investments we have worked so hard to earn. We all have graduate degrees, some of us own businesses, and some have very well-paying jobs, but we could not manage to save or to buy homes like other people our age have done.

We just felt stuck, unable to do anything because Father hurt Mother and then left the family, and we have never been the same since. What a waste! If we could have focused on the positive things in our lives, we might have achieved more. Fortunately, the future is not carved in stone. We have learned to expect more from ourselves and not to doubt. Doing this allows us to trust the Lord to give us what he sees fit. We are in expectant joy, which is there for all those who seek it.

We now realize that a major key to success, joy and happiness in life is to be completely free of guilt, resentment and self-pity. My desire is to inspire and motivate others to look at their lives, and see what mental holds they have, if any.

I wish to have them look within themselves and give everything they can to fight these inner demons so they may one day have nothing holding them back from living the lives they want. Life cannot deny itself to anyone who gives his or her all. The Bible says, "Seek, and you shall find." It's time to get out of the victim mentality and set our sights on greatness.

I love one song that I play a lot on my gospel motivation radio show every Sunday on www.visiosnsfm.com

The main lyrics in the chorus are sung as follows:

Mumwe nemumwe anondomira nezvake kudenga" Meaning that *"We will all stand individually in judgement before The Lord"*.

It is therefore up to each of us to take that step towards greatness. Mark 9:23 says,

"All things are possible to him that believeth."

As written in Matthew 17:23, the Bible says,

"If we have faith ... nothing shall be impossible."
Matthew 9:29 tells us,

"According to your faith so shall it be unto you."

It is critical to think, speak, visualize and take action towards what you want. Rather than speaking negativity, focus on what is not working and think of ways to fix it. I challenge you to practice thinking positively. It works.

I will leave you with a story told in the book The Power of Positive Thinking by Norman Vincent Peale. He talks about one boy who was frozen with fear when he was about to go on a trapeze bar. He could see himself falling to the ground, and that frightened him to death.

The instructor looked at this young man and said, "Son, you can do it. Throw your heart over the bar and your body will follow." What the instructor meant was that if this young man could see himself leap over the bar, he could make himself succeed at what he had envisioned.

This is true with everything else; when you force your heart to be filled with whatever it is that you desire, where you want to go, what you want to do, or what you want to be, the energy you will need to make this vision true will come. It's about expecting the best out of every situation.

It's about following our spiritual principles; believe in what the Lord can do and blessings will start flowing.

I continue to be amazed by people who limit themselves and minimize what they are capable of achieving. There are no limits, because our help comes from the one who created the earth, us, and the whole universe. If he says "Yes," who can be against us? It's time we all pick ourselves up and pursue the lives we dream of living.

Lessons Learned

(1) **Gratitude.** I have learned to be grateful for what I have in anticipation of what is to come. When I feel that I am putting myself in a victim's role, I like to ask myself: "Does someone else on this planet have it worse than me?" Having the opportunity to counsel and coach others through their despair has allowed me to see my struggles as minimal compared to what I hear. We pray with Mother all the time, and we acknowledge that we have much to be grateful for in our lives.

(2) **Forgiveness.** It's easy to get wrapped up in thinking that forgiveness is just something you "should do," rather than something you "must do." But forgiving can be extremely beneficial to everyone willing to let go. We have finally come to realize that we need to release all our feelings of

resentment, anger, and pain related to Father's choices and embrace them. As Catherine Ponder says:

"When you hold resentment toward another, you are bound to that person or condition by an emotional link that is stronger than steel. Forgiveness is the only way to dissolve that link and get free."

We have allowed our father to control all our lives emotionally for a long time, and now it is time to release him and take charge of our own lives. As long as we don't forgive him, we will always be negatively linked to him. That is not what we want. We want him to be as free of us as we are free of him. He will have to go through his own lessons before he can come to the point where he, too, can forgive and move on. For now, we forgive him, and we forgive ourselves.

Forgiving doesn't mean forgetting; it simply means freeing ourselves from the emotional link that has held us so strongly, inflicting so much suffering on all of us. This has resulted in a great deal of inner turmoil, affecting not only our loved ones, but all those around us, too.

(3)   **Turning the pain into power,** by focusing outward and helping someone else. My goal as a messenger of Hope is to add value to your life. By making myself available to talk to others about victimhood in polygamists' wives and children, I foster conversation and growth that has brought much-needed healing to all of us.

(4)   **Give yourself a break.** We all have failed and made mistakes; no one is perfect. We have given Mother a forum where she can vent and tell her story. I don't think we gave Father as much space to tell his side of the story. We cannot move back the hands of time, but both Mother and Father are alive as of this writing, and it is time they take back this issue and resolve it between them.

If they need to forgive each other, they should ask each other for forgiveness so that they can give each other a final break from the emotional hold polygamy has over each of them. Then, they need to accept what has happened as adults and call it a day. We, their children, are stepping back, taking the lessons learned, and guiding our families toward becoming respectful and loving beings.

I have realized that my parents have both been influential, one way or another. Dad has always believed that I was capable of doing more. He has always believed I can be a person of influence. I thank you, Dad, for your belief, your guidance, and your example. I now see why you burned the candle at both ends when you owned "Amalgamated Estate Agents" and the Kudzanayi store in Chiwundura.

I realize now that I have learned all the confidence and business sense I have from my parents. Mother has been my stage and speaking coach. She has critiqued my speeches and given me praise when I do well. She has traveled with me to speaking engagements in churches, retreats, seminars, and workshops in and out of the United States.

Her presence and guidance have been a constant blessing. I am more confident and assertive when she is around, because I know she will have something to say after each presentation. She has been my cheerleader, my prayer warrior, and my biggest supporter. My prayer was to make sure her tears did not flow in vain; I wanted to make her proud. I have prayed for the Lord to use me so that

Mother can see and feel his hand in her children's lives. She has said it many times, *"Mwari munondida zvininyadzisa,"* meaning 'Lord you love me Thriving Beyond measure, it's even embarrassing to know the love you have for me.' She deserves the love, happiness and joy she has worked so hard to gain back. The lesson for me and today's woman is, we do not have to settle, we do not have to stay for the children.

A Dose of Motivation

Happiness and joy is what you get when you decide to 'let go and let God.' Deciding to run your own race in life allows you to create the best possible life for you. Despite everything you have endured, you still can choose to do your best, create the best, and achieve the best in your life.

Just laughing, having people or a person you can talk to, is very important, because your happiness is very important, both physically and mentally. When you are in a happy emotional space, you can more easily accomplish whatever it is you seek, and you are able to see miracles manifest in your life. Happiness and joy are key to achieving what we want.

- **Try your best to be calm at all times.** Don't allow small things to stress you. When something big stresses you, feel the stress, acknowledge how big it is, and then refuse to let it stress you further. When you miss an opportunity, don't be upset over it the whole day. When you have been violated or when you have been hurt, don't let it upset your whole life. Don't let your negative experiences block your enjoyment of your blessings.

- **Lighten up your mood.** If you are feeling very stressed out, try to lighten up your mood by doing whatever makes you feel more relaxed. I love music, so I listen to music. I also take long bubble baths or get massages. All these activities stimulate a part of my brain that releases what we call endorphins, which are essential chemicals that trigger feelings of happiness and overall relaxation. Find out what helps you relax—long walks, reading a good book, playing a board game with friends—and do it.

- **Relationships.** I am so grateful for having the close relationship I have with my siblings; we are very close. It is such a joy to be around them, and I know I can talk to them about anything at any time of day or night. We rotate cooking on weekends and just spend time together laughing, eating, and relaxing with each other. It was both our parents' wishes that we would stay close when we started moving to the USA.

Seeing us, I have no doubt this is a blessing far Thriving Beyond the tears they have both shed each in their own way and time. We love our father and have a great relationship with him because he is the only father we know, however mother now knows she has choices and it's ok to choose.

- **Take nature walks.** It is true that exercising in any form opens you up to respond better to feelings of happiness and joy. I live by an ocean, so I take nature walks with Mother; the breeze just blows away any worries I might have.

Having green plants in your home and making sure your home is neat and bright also creates a happy, delightful ambience. You deserve it; go forth and live a life full of purpose. It's possible for all of us to have a life as good as, or better than, our dreams.

10

From Pain To Power - Bruised But Not Broken

"Sometimes the cards we are dealt are not always fair. However, you must keep smiling and moving on." Tom Jackson

"You are responsible for your life. You can't keep blaming somebody else for your dysfunction. Life is really about moving on."

Oprah Winfrey

Chapter 10
From Pain To Power - Bruised But Not broken

It is very refreshing to know that we can always have a second, third, or fourth chance (in truth, even more chances than that) to start our lives over. It is empowering to see women in general having a voice, pursuing their education, running their own businesses and acknowledging that God has given them a vision of greatness and they deserve every blessing they seek.

The telephone prayer lines have, in my humble opinion, been a blessing to many. I am excited when I see that women in general, be it us African, or African-American, American, etc. are wasting no time in constructing and following their dreams. They all are walking along their path and building the road towards success.

Many others, however, are still confined by fear that prevents them from moving towards their dreams. Many cannot find the strength to move Thriving Beyond these fears. I believe God has already given us the authority to take action, as seen in the gifts—our blessings—that he has empowered us with; we only need to take those first steps and he will help us the rest of the way. It is always exciting when I conduct workshops or when I am a guest speaker, hearing women be passionate about their relationship with God, but also hearing that they have shared that passion through their businesses, through their work and through the successes of their children.

All these women and men are champions of God's will. I would like to share Kirk Franklin's song that ministers to my heart at all times when I am in doubt, or regressing back to the complaining and stagnancy. We need to know that God is in the process of bringing us through a period called time.

Once we understand that life is a process, and then we don't judge people in the middle of their journey. My own process teaches me that because God has been patient with me, I need to be patient with myself, with others, and with God. Because God has given me some space, then I need to give others some space.

Because He has given me grace, I am obligated to show grace to those whom I work with. I believe it is possible to rise from pain to find both power and purpose; I believe we can move from a state of being crushed and broken to being brave and courageous.

The pain that we all endure now and then is a part of the process of life that teaches us to be strong. These pains also teach us to rely on God alone to bring us peace.

I am a certified trainer and coach of the 'Feel the Fear and Do It Anyway' training sessions created by Susan Jeffers. In these training sessions are life-changing lessons on how to overcome the fears that keep us in our broken, bruised state.

If we are to become whole then we need to work on recognizing and overcoming the fears that get in our way. In short, Susan Jeffers explains how we handle fear as we move from pain to power, from helplessness to choice, from depression to excitement, and from paralysis to action.

The way she explains it makes it clear that the secret in dealing with fear is to act as though you always have a choice. It's amazing what happens when you decide that you are going to do something or achieve something despite the fear. You quickly find that you have the power to do what is necessary.

As of today, start listening to yourself and work on eliminating the thoughts that have prevented you from receiving the blessings you are praying for. Remember, you do have a choice, even if the choice you make is to wait where you are and watch for a better opportunity to act.

I realize that we are not the persons we used to be. Process has a way of changing who we are. Thank God we are not what we used to be, yet still on the path toward becoming what we are going to be. I don't know what happens to us when we are in the fire, facing challenges—we forget, we panic, we become hurt and we resent others. There will be trials and tribulations that will befall us as believers. Victory is ours if we can take a step back and acknowledge the presence of the Lord or higher power through these difficult times.

As believers, if we take the time to trust in him, to endure the dark days, we can still have peace, even in the midst of the storm. As a matter of fact, we need to continue to glorify our God through the peace and confidence he shows us in the face of adversity.

I have never seen him forsake the righteous, therefore we need to remain in him and have him help us to find our peace and understanding and to move Thriving Beyond the   tears.
Since we know that trouble will come our way one day,

that the troubles will come whether we are prepared or not, and how we deal with them is what matters. There is no Saint when it comes to facing challenges and problems in life. I look at Mother, who is so peaceful because of prayer and stewardship. Her prayers, my prayers, and our belief in all things possible have helped. The telephone prayer lines and the church have helped me tremendously as well.

Fellow sisters and mothers, It is very important that we find best ways to deal with our innermost pains. For my mother the Divine Intervention has been the prayer lines and church. Mother, has been such a good inspiration and motivation as she can relate to this, and she, too, has felt the same defeats. I feel we have all been, at one point or another, struck down but not destroyed.

 I feel that Mother represents a lot of women around the World who are in a battle of the emotions right now. They have never talked about their innermost pain, their embarrassment, their fears and ambitions. Many have lost their lives in the name of polygamy, but Mother has endured and survived.

The stress has caused many people to endure high blood pressure, HIV/AIDS, untreated depression, and heart attacks, all of which have resulted in the untimely loss of life or terminal illness for some people. She has overcome the worst of the worst and lived to see God answer her prayer, to have her tears be a blessing to her children. I too, have come through many storms, but I'm still standing. As my girl Leysa de Govia-Purcell affectionately said when she heard of this memoir project, "Stem! I am so happy for you. If anyone deserves happiness, you do! It's been a long road; I'm so proud of you. Hugs and kisses, girl!"

My peace comes from Mother who continues to pray and cry tears of joy, asking God to continue to shower me and my siblings with his never ending love and blessings. In Matthew 28:20 Jesus says,"...lo I am with you always, even to the end of the age. I love hearing this as I know that He is Able. Like the weather some days are good some are bad, but through it all I have to remember that I can do and be everywhere you soar.

"For the eyes of the Lord run to and from throughout the whole earth, to show himself strong on behalf of those whose heart is loyal to Him....." (2 Chronicles 16:9)

I can only say that my mother deserves every laugh and every bit of peace of mind she can get, now that she is here in the USA reaping the rewards of her prayers and faithfulness. She now more often than I care to count, will come into my room and say "Thank you for making me so proud and happy. If I die today please know that I am at peace, I am happy, mine eyes have seen, I wanted God to keep me so that I can see, the end of all this, I have seen."

It is difficult to hear, but I am consoled, as I worry all the time if she is now at peace, if she has received the ultimate gift of all, a peace of mind. With that I am thinking of her now feeling a sense of unsurpassed peace which is the absence of mental stress or anxiety, depression.

I am thinking of a sense of peace that is the presence of serenity, calm, quiet, comfort of mind, and deep inner peace. I see her relaxed, I see her laughing and I have no doubt she has received the gift of God's gift of peace.

I don't hear her reiterating her pain over and over as she did before, I don't see her panic if my father sends a text saying "tell your mother I am selling the house".

I have witnessed Mother go through the following emotions and changes in her fight for peace, and understanding Thriving Beyond her tears.

Accept what is

She has accepted what is. She now knows that there is only so much we can affect or change in our lives, painful moments will happen whether you are good or bad. Your being a divine woman does not exempt you from painful moments. What we cannot change, what we cannot influence no matter what, should not be a concern to us.

This is what I noticed that before she focused and lingered on things my father did, his wife did to her when they were in her home, the pain she felt from relatives who betrayed her by accepting the other wives to be in her home. She had no control over why they did this, I see now she has let go.

All relatives in their own way heave spoken to Mother and apologized, which is quite humbling on her part. She now will openly say why worry about my father's behavior, something that all the worrying in the world will not change?

Why care about what other people think of her when she is not even sure what it is they are actually thinking? She has accepted what is, gaining herself an inner peace like no other.

Meditate

Even though she will not call it meditation. I have seen Mother take time to be quiet, relaxing with no outside influences. I have seen her watch shows that are soothing and relaxing on television. I have seen her refrain from taking calls to relax her mind, and then call once she is in good space. She treasures her peacefulness, which is a big step for her. She deserves the peace and relaxation, I tell her to enjoy the pension, she has worked hard.

Spend time in nature

Mother loves water so we walk all the time by the beach or sit out on our patio and watch birds, look at nature from our patio. She is an avid exercise freak; I call her so you will find her stretching watching a yoga program or exercising with an exercise session on television.

Learn the power of a smile and letting go

Mother loves the phone; I have fun watching her acting like a kid whenever her friends or my siblings call. She is happy to talk to all, so if you ever call her and she talks to you for a second then tells you she has to take another call, please don't be offended, she has no telephone etiquette. Mother does not want to miss any calls, her goal is to just say hello so that everyone know they are acknowledged. My goal and prayer is to make sure that she gets what she wants; she goes wherever she wants to go and enjoys whatever she wants to enjoy. I am at her service, she is my QUEEN. Every mother deserves that QUEEN treatment, especially if they sacrifice their own happiness as my mother did.

Care about others

I am yet to know anybody who has unconditional love for everyone as my mother has. She has no discrimination that you are not a relative or her child; she genuinely loves and cares for everyone. She will tell you herself that she holds no grudges; she has no hate bone in her. I believe her. From the time we were young, we brought our friends home and they were hooked to both our parents, Mother has not changed. Friends will come to my house and before I know it they are coming back again and again to see mummy.

She now provides telephonic counseling and prayer to many prayer line partners and friends from back home. She genuinely prays for each person as if she is praying for one of her own. Such unconditional love is to be hailed; thank you for that lesson, Mother. I have no doubt I do what I do from the heart because I have the best teacher in the world. The other day I broke one of my teeth and had to emergency extraction. I cancelled all appointments except one elderly lady did not check her messages and went to my office for her counseling appointment. She called me from my office and from her voice I could tell she was in distress.

I got up, mouth swollen and drove to my office with a scarf around my mouth. I knew she needed to talk more than I needed to nurse my swollen jaw. All I could think of is how unselfish Mother has been with her life. It was one of the best sessions we have had with that lady, my joy and peace comes from seeing my patients get relief, and that she did.

When I help other people, I stop focusing on my so-called problems and realize that my life isn't so bad after all. This rids my entire being of all the stress and feelings of overwhelm. There is great peace and wisdom in thinking and caring about other people, which we are blind to when we are too deep within our own selfish ways.

Never lose hope

Mother has been a champion through it all. She has learned to trust in Jesus and in turn taught to totally trust in the Lord. He is an all knowing God; he knows where he is taking us. If my father had not remarried, got rid of me and send me to the USA so that he could bring his next wife to our home.

There is a saying in shona that goes:

"Ayambutsa zongororo, ari yambutsa zvamuchose nokuti harichadzoke, harogone kuyambuka rega."

When my father got rid of me and send me to the USA, it was my blessing. This was God's way of changing the whole course of my family's life. It's been a blessing looking back and seeing how we have been blessed through it all. It's been humbling to see God's hand at work, he never forgot Mother's prayers, when we thought he had forgotten why was this happening, and he knew his plans were bigger than our eyes could see.

I am the voice of Hope when I am on radio presenting my gospel show "Let's praise him/Ngatimurumbidzei /asimdhumiseni on www.visionsfm.com.

I have every reason to praise him, because he knows my heart, he knows how much I want to serve him and bring the hope I have known to others. My name Sithembile means Hope.

Hope is something you can never afford to lose. With hope you always have a path towards peace. Whenever we get too stressed out and overwhelmed within our own life, we forget that hope. We forget that the sun always shines after a rainy day, and that this is merely a bump in the road. I find immense peace in just knowing, deep within my heart, that everything will be ok.

With hope, I now know that whatever is seemingly terrible for right now is only temporary and that soon enough, things will be just fine. This lifts off all of that negativity from my entire being, and I feel better pretty much instantly.

Live in the present moment

What a journey, seeing Mother living in the present is priceless. It's interesting, that most of the time, what we worry about is relating to something either in the past, or something that hasn't happened.

Mother went through the struggle of relating to the past for a very long time. Living in the present moment erases all such thoughts. Why worry about something in the past that we cannot ever change?

Thriving Beyond the Tears - *Bruised and Never Broken* | Dr. Stem Mahlatini

She has accepted that she cannot change what happened, the love between her and father is a new love. What they had is no longer the same but the respect can be restored because of us children, we are a product of them both. We love both dearly and we would not be without the other.

We can take care of both; Dad will be taken care of where he is or, if he chooses to come here, he too deserves and will receive the same royal treatment. They both sacrificed a lot for us to be where we are. We love them both. The bible in Deuteronomy 5:16 says ""Honor your father and your mother, as the LORD your God has commanded you, so that you may live long and that it may go well with you in the land the LORD your God is giving you".

Mother and I used to be two people who worried all the time, to the point where we both had trouble sleeping. Once we learned to live in the present moment, to determinate between what we can and cannot control and controlling those things we could, we were at peace, we stopped thinking about the past and focused more on today and our potential future.

Mother is definitely at peace and in turn my life is definitely more at peace because of the sense of peace I see in her. have let go of the notion that it's my role as the

Thriving Beyond the Tears - *Bruised and Never Broken* | Dr. Stem Mahlatini

oldest child to ensure that with God's help and guidance both my parents learn to dance Thriving Beyond their tears, yes their tears. I am responsible for me and they are responsible for how they choose to live their lives. Somehow I believe there were many nights my father shed tears and no one will ever know.

He is a very loving father and at some point was a loving husband to Mother. I know God will see that they both will leave to see his glory and join hands celebrating the successes their children have accomplished and will continue to accomplish. I have no doubt they are proud. I am Free.

Lessons Learned

I have been through many tearful moments and overcame. As believers we must face the reality that we will face many hard trials. Yet, we can face each storm with the calm assurance that though we have been battered, we are never defeated.

Though we have been victimized we can choose a life that is free of the emotional hold of victimhood. I've been to hell and back at times. Mother has had it even worse, but s h e   i s   s t i l l   s t a n d i n g .

It's Time for Our Best Life, It's Time For Our Blessings. For God, who said, 'Let light shine out of darkness,' made his light shine in our hearts to give us the light of the knowledge of the glory of God in the face of Christ.

A Dose of Motivation

- Are you living the life you love? Are you doing what you love and loving what you do?

- Are you doing EXACTLY the kind of work that makes you want to leap out of bed each morning, excited to begin a new day?

- Does your work satisfy a deep need to express yourself, your talents, your values, and your unique and precious gifts?

- Does your work allow for a balanced life – one that leaves time for family and friends, for exercise or hobbies, and for yourself?

- Are you in a fulfilling relationship? Are you doing your part to ensure a balance?

Remember that you deserve the best and whether you see it or not, the potter is at hand weaving your life. Though the answers sometimes appear to be taking way too long, wait on the Lord for he shall make sure your destiny is fulfilled. We will cry tears at one time or another, however I want to remind you that you owe it to yourself to live the life you were created to have. Wishing you a blessed and Happy Life.

In Thriving Beyond The Tears, may you Find Your Own Hope, Happiness and joy.

Update October 2015

Many have asked whatever happened to the house? What happened to your dad? Here is an update.

Looking back at 50, I am in awe of my dad's steadfast character. He has never been one to conform to what people want of him, he has always stood for what he believed and waited until a time he can get things done his way. He never budged and both his wives and children are now settled in the USA and doing well.

My father signed the house to my mother. She still lives in the house. There are times when you have to let go and allow yourself to direct and create your own life regardless of your past and your parents' choices. I also have grown and realize after much therapy and coaching that I am responsible of how I choose to live my life. I am responsible of how I choose to listen and react to those silent whispers of my heart and soul. In the end, we are meant to choose peace, joy, happiness, however we can create it for ourselves. My father had his way and my mother had her way.

Believe it or not mother is now in a very good place where she too understands that she had choices that she did not take because of her values and beliefs. By writing this book, I have chosen to break the cycle, to allow those who are ready to be free, to be free from feeling trapped or limited by cultural beliefs, family beliefs or personal beliefs. In the end, you have the power to free yourself, only you can free yourself.

Living Thriving Beyond the Tears will require work on yourself, it will require time and it will require monetary investment. The result is a happier joyful and free spirited you. I am all that and more.

Be Encouraged.

In Thriving Beyond The Tears, I await the day we will have a family Reunion with all wives, children in one place, village, resort, mansion and celebrate the blood we share. We are all one after all, we share the same father.

About The Author
Dr. Stem. Sithembile Mahlatini

Originally from Zimbabwe, Africa, Dr. Sithembile "Stem" Mahlatini is president and owner of Global Coaching & Consulting Services, LLC (GC&C) in Swampscott and Salem, Massachusetts, and she is also President and Founder of Women & Youth Empowerment Seminars (WYES).

She is a Motivational/Inspirational Speaker, a Certified Life-Career Coach, Author, and Licensed Psychotherapist. She is also a Co-Author of Seven Books on Women empowerment through the Professional Woman Network. She resides in Boston, Massachusetts.

Dr. Mahlatini life's work is to inspire, motivate and educate others through her books, seminars, workshops, counselling and coaching services. Dr. Mahlatini offers people practical advice on how to tap into their limitless power to change their lives, overcome roadblocks and aspire to be better than the circumstances that surround them.

Her lifelong goal is to continue to empower and inspire all people to be their best authentic self at home, work and business. Her motto is, "Each day is an opportunity to change your life and bring out the new you."

Dr. Mahlatini attended Nova Southeastern University where she earned a Doctorate Degree in Education, specializing in Organizational Development and leadership. She is also a graduate of Boston University where she earned a Master's Degree in Social Work, and she is licensed as a psychotherapist in Massachusetts and Florida.

She is also a Certified Speaker, Trainer and Coach as a Founding Member of the John Maxwell Team, where adding Value to the People is key. Her John Maxwell Trainings include:

A)   Put your Dreams to the Test
B)   Becoming a person of Influence
C)   Everyone Communicates but Few Connect
D)   How to be a Real Success
E)   The 15 Invaluable Laws of Growth

She is a member of the Back Talk Toastmasters club, the Professional Woman Network, The National Speakers

Association and the National Association of Social Workers.

Dr. Stem recent appearances include being a guest speaker at a Women in Network (WIN) event, where she spoke on "Own Your Direction;" a life coaching workshop through the Lynn, Massachusetts Chamber of Commerce; the Christian Fellowship International Ministries where she spoke on "The Power of Praise;" a workshop for the South Shore Businesswomen on "Coping with Grief in the Workplace" the Victory Family Church International women's conference where she conducted a two day workshop on "Possibilities: Turning Dreams into Reality; The ZAWAC "Zimbabwe Women Abroad Club" women's Conference in Atlanta, GA where she spoke on "Bruised But Not Broken" and the Women of Dominion, Indiana GA where she spoke on "How to start and own a business" and "Feel the Fear and Do It Anyway workshop.

Dr Stem is also an Employee Assistance Professional (EAP) Provider who specializes in wellness programs that include:
1.   Coping with Work and Family Stress
2.   Depression and Anxiety in the Workplace
3.   Self-confidence in the Workplace –being managed and managing others

4. Compassion Fatigue: When the Helping Profession Hurts
5. The Professional Supervisor, Manager and Leader

In addition to speaking and training, she counsels and coaches clients in her private practice office in Salem, Massachusetts. She serves clientele throughout the United States, Africa, the Caribbean, the United Kingdom, and Australia through one-on-one telephone coaching, skype and video. One of her dear to heart and passion is music especially gospel music and reggae music.

Dr. Stem is available as a retreat speaker and trainer who offers onsite employee diversity, morale trainings, and one-on-one coaching. Consultations are conducted in person, by telephone or on-site.

Her programs include:
- Beyond The Tears-Bruised But Not Broken
- It's Time to Shift: From Fear to Faith
- The Power of Prayer and Belief
- Possibilities – Turning Dreams into Reality
- Change Your Thinking – Change Your Life
- The Rollercoaster Ride is Over! Handling Emotions
- Handling Stress: Sink, Swim or Float & More

Below are some commendations from Family and Friends to help you envision the personality and character of your next guest speaker, coach and trainer, DrStem Mahlatini. A God sent angel, who puts others first before herself, a hard worker, dedicated, motivator and above all she is caring lovable, passionate and royal.

She is a leader in so many ways an inspirational individual who thrives to be on top and always dreaming big. As a sister i couldn't have ask for anyone else because she is the best sister who makes everyone around her want to be somebody. stay blessed auntie love you Always, Mavis Nyagura Guy

Our best friend should be an easy thing to do; however, more than 20 years of memory make it difficult to find a starting point. My friend, Stem, is a complex, yet simple woman whom I have grown to know and enjoy being around. She is someone who lives life with a passion and fire inside.

About 23 years ago, Stem and I (Saru) met and became instantly connected as friends. Almost immediately we became good friends. As a transparent individual, it was easy to feel her faith, her love for family and her generosity for others. To know her is to love her. As a friend, she has always been very supportive; she always listens and to me and has always been ready to render her advice.

Upon first meeting her, you would be convinced that is a quiet and shy person, but that is only half the story. A few minutes in her company; however, lead you to conclude that she is an intelligent, direct, kind, nurturing, and generous person. In some ways we are so alike, while in others, we are so different. As peculiar as it sounds, it is those similarities and differences that have made our friendship work. More than anything else, I am in awe with her desire to make others feel important.

Mary Kay Ash once said, "I believe that you will make every day incredible just by what you exude in your eyes, your handshake and your friendly spirit." I believe those words were written for Stem. If you were to meet her, you too would walk away convinced that what I write is accurate. You too would be convinced that she has what it takes to put others at ease.

She always gives her undivided attention to those whom she engages in conversation. Stem understands Mary Kay's philosophy. She practices that philosophy daily. Her accomplishments are a testament to the way she leads her life.

Over the years, we have had our ups and downs, but we have always spoken the to each other. That does not mean; however, that she never makes mistakes. Whenever she does, she is never too big to apologize. Even when she apologizes, she understands that "apologizing does not always mean you are wrong and the other person is right. It simply means you value the relationship more than your ego" (author unknown). She holds no grudges because she does not believe the extra weight is worth carrying.

Although she is focused on fulfilling her dreams, she values the easy pace of life. That easy going nature is visible the moment you get to know her. Consequently, she places more value on people than on things. Therefore, she is a very giving person (almost to a fault). If she has it, she will give it away with all her heart without expecting something in return. In short, Stem can be described as a self-less individual, someone who is not too proud to give away the shirt on her back to someone with a greater need.

Stem's life is built in her faith in God. She never stops thanking God for her blessings, even when things go wrong for her. Her spirituality keeps her grounded. Over the years, we have done a lot together, been through a lot together. Through all the ups and downs, the highs and low, our friendship has remained solid. I believe that she has allowed every struggle in her life to mold and shape her into the person she is today. She is the epitome of "What don't kill you makes you stronger."

That does not mean; however, she is a perfect individual. The good thing is though, she knows it and acknowledges the fact that we all fall short of God's glory. Over the years, she has had to disassociate with those who have discredited her and learned how to surround herself with positive people, people who bring out the best in her. She hangs her heart on the words of John Maxwell, "A best friend is he who brings out the best in you."

There is so much more that I would like to share about my dear friend, Stem, but because of my desire to leave room for others, I will limit my musings to the impact that she has gad on me. Stem, I want you to know that nurturing a friendship like the one we have is difficult. As you know, I am not perfect.

I will continue to make mistakes and maybe even hurt your feelings. Amidst my indiscretions; however, always remember that I love you with all my heart. I am proud of the person you have become.

I admire your strength and your desire to make a difference in the lives of others. You have set an example not just for me, but for your siblings and for women in business. God will carry you through. He will see that you achieve every goal and every dream that you have set for yourself. I thank God every day for bringing you into my life.

I couldn't have asked for a better friend, a better "sister." Thank you so much for being my friend and a mom to my son, Matthew. My life is blessed with you in it. Proverbs 18:15 says, "The heart of the prudent acquires knowledge, and the ear of the wise seeks knowledge." Over the years, you have done that and you have stuck with it.

Keep your faith my dear one and remember that, "If you are too busy for God then it is time to change your schedule," (Joyce Meyer). People love you, and listen to you because you make time to reach and touch others. According to Joel Osteen, "Everyday try to find someone you can complement someone you can build up.

It is amazing how your words of encouragement bless others." I know you could have written those words yourself; you have mastered them.

Keep on keeping on my friend. May God bless you above and beyond. You are truly a blessing, not just to me, but to those who have grown to know and love you.
I love you always my dear

Your Best Friend "Chiraxha"
--- aka Saru Furusa Walsh

For individual and/or group life coaching, contact Dr. Stem Mahlatini at:
(781) 254-1602,
email drstemahlatini@gmail.com o
or log onto her website at...

www.globalcoachconsulting.com,

...and register for her life-changing women and youth empowerment seminars

References:

Dr. Phillip C. McGraw Self Matters: Creating Your Life from the Inside Out

DrStem
Teen Parent Empowerment Seminars - TPES

Thriving Beyond the Tears - *Bruised and Never Broken* | Dr. Stem Mahlatini

www.ingramcontent.com/pod-product-compliance
Lightning Source LLC
Chambersburg PA
CBHW060316030426
42336CB00011B/1075